Some Things Are Not Common

To Kyle, My friend,
May God's Grace find
you and Keep you!
Remember to be careful not
to call the things God has made
Holy, Common! Acts 10:13

Some Things Are Not Common

Dr. David W. Weimer

Library of Congress Control Number:		2011961272
ISBN:	Hardcover	978-1-4653-0931-0
	Softcover	978-1-4653-0930-3
	Ebook	978-1-4653-0932-7

To order additional copies of this book, contact:
Xlibris Corporation
1-888-795-4274
www.Xlibris.com
Orders@Xlibris.com
106390

CONTENTS

ACKNOWLEDGEMENTS 7

INTRODUCTION 9

CHAPTER 1   YHWH 13

CHAPTER 2   "HALLOWED BE THY NAME" 24

CHAPTER 3   JESUS CHRIST 33

CHAPTER 4   WORD OF GOD 38

CHAPTER 5   TITHE 46

CHAPTER 6   SAINTS 51

CHAPTER 7   SIGNS, WONDERS, AND MIRACLES 59

CHAPTER 8   COVENANTS AND PROMISES 63

CHAPTER 9   REDEMPTION 66

CHAPTER 10   MANKIND 69

CHAPTER 11   FAITH 71

CONCLUSION 77

ENDNOTES 79

ACKNOWLEDGEMENTS

I am grateful to the numerous words of encouragement from those who first heard these ideas in sermonic form. It is because of their urging and the urging of the Holy Spirit that I wrote this manuscript. I further thank my beloved wife, Sandra, for her willingness to encourage me over the past fifty years. Her belief in me encouraged me to believe in myself and trust God to make up the difference. She also made the final proofreading of the document. I also thank my students of twenty-five years for their hunger to learn. Their hunger forced me to study and prepare hard for each class.

I would like to especially thank my neighbor and fellow teacher for the past six years, Pastor Edward Maher, for reading the partially finished document and making suggestions for its improvement. Also, I acknowledge the two young men, Zack Lorton and D. Mark Weimer, who labored over the completed document to proofread it.

Finally, my greatest acknowledgement is to my friends, Jesus and Holy Spirit, who have taught me to respect the Holy things. I thank them for their faithful discipline and loving grace and mercy over the decades of my life.

INTRODUCTION

When God touches or cleanses something it is no longer ordinary or common. He has transferred it from the domain of the common or profane to the domain of the extraordinary and holy. An open vision caused Peter to become aware of this in Acts chapter ten. He saw it illustrated in vivid form before his eyes. God offered him lunch on a sheet. All that Peter had to do was to slaughter it and prepare it. Because of his prejudicial religious views he failed to receive what God had provided. God used this situation to teach him that human beings and all other things cleansed by Him are not common or unclean. It was a startling realization for Peter and it changed his life and the Jerusalem Church. Whenever someone encounters the uncommon things, those things will become an instrument of change for him. When one mishandles these things they bring him face to face with the correction of God and even His judgment.

Acts 10:1-48 (KJV): There was a certain man in Caesarea called Cornelius, a centurion of the band called the Italian band, A devout man, and one that feared God with all his house, which gave much alms to the people, and prayed to God alway. He saw in a vision evidently about the ninth hour of the day an angel of God coming in to him, and saying unto him, Cornelius. And when he looked on him, he was afraid, and said, What is it, Lord? And he said unto him, Thy prayers and thine alms are come up for a memorial before God. And now send men to Joppa, and call for one Simon, whose surname is Peter: He lodgeth with one Simon a tanner, whose house is by the sea side: he shall tell thee what thou oughtest to do. And when the angel which spake unto Cornelius was departed, he called two of his household servants, and a devout soldier of them that waited on him continually; And when he had declared all these things unto them, he sent them to Joppa. On the morrow, as they went on their journey, and drew nigh unto the city, Peter went up upon the housetop to pray about the sixth hour: And he became very hungry, and would have eaten: but while they made ready, he fell into a trance, And saw heaven opened, and a certain vessel descending unto him, as it had been a great sheet knit at the four corners, and let down to the earth: Wherein were all manner of fourfooted beasts of the earth, and wild beasts, and creeping things, and fowls of the air. And there came a voice to him, Rise, Peter; kill, and eat. But Peter said, Not so, Lord; for I have never eaten any thing that is common or unclean[1]. And the voice spake unto him again the second time, What God hath cleansed, that call not thou common. This was done thrice: and the vessel was received up again into heaven. Now while Peter doubted in himself what this vision which he had seen should mean, behold, the men which were sent from Cornelius had made inquiry for Simon's house, and stood before the gate, And called, and asked whether Simon, which was surnamed Peter, were lodged there. While Peter thought on the vision, the Spirit said unto him, Behold, three men seek thee. Arise therefore, and get thee down, and go with them, doubting nothing: for I have sent them. Then Peter went down to the men which were sent unto him from Cornelius; and said, Behold, I am he whom ye seek: what is the cause wherefore ye are come? And they said, Cornelius the centurion, a just man, and one that feareth God, and of good report among all the nation of the Jews, was warned from God by an holy angel to send for thee into his house, and to hear words of thee. Then called he them in, and lodged them. And on the morrow Peter went away with them, and certain brethren from Joppa accompanied him. And the morrow after they entered into Caesarea. And Cornelius waited for them, and had called together his kinsmen and near friends. And as Peter was coming in, Cornelius met him, and fell down at his feet, and worshipped him. But Peter took him up, saying, Stand up; I myself also am a man. And as he talked with him, he went in, and found many that were come together. And he said unto them, Ye know how that it is an unlawful thing for a man that is a Jew to keep company, or come unto one of another nation; but God hath shewed me that I should not call any man common or unclean. Therefore came I unto you without gainsaying, as soon as I was sent for: I ask therefore for what intent ye have sent for me? And Cornelius said, Four days ago I was fasting until this hour; and at the ninth hour I prayed in my house, and, behold, a man stood before me in bright clothing, And said, Cornelius, thy prayer is heard, and thine alms are had in remembrance in the sight of God. Send therefore to Joppa, and call hither Simon, whose surname is Peter; he is lodged in the house of one Simon a tanner by the sea side: who, when he cometh, shall speak unto thee. Immediately therefore I sent to thee; and thou hast well done that thou art come. Now therefore are we all here present before God, to hear all things that are commanded thee of God. Then Peter opened his mouth, and said, Of a truth I perceive that God is no respecter of persons: But in every nation he that feareth him, and worketh righteousness, is accepted with him. The word which God sent unto the children of Israel, preaching peace by Jesus Christ: (he is Lord of all:) That word, I say, ye know, which was published throughout all Judaea, and began from Galilee, after the baptism which John preached; How God anointed Jesus of Nazareth with the Holy Ghost and with power: who went about *doing good, and healing all that were oppressed of the devil; for God was with him. And we are witnesses of all things which he did both in the land of the Jews, and in Jerusalem; whom they slew and hanged on a tree: Him God raised up the third day, and shewed him openly; Not to all the people, but unto witnesses chosen before of God, even to us, who did eat and drink with him after he rose from the dead. And he commanded us to preach unto the people, and to testify that it is he which was ordained of God to be the Judge of quick and dead. To him give all the prophets witness, that through his name whosoever believeth in him shall receive remission of sins. While Peter yet spake these words, the Holy Ghost fell on all them which heard the word. And they of the circumcision which believed were astonished, as many as came with Peter, because that on the Gentiles also was poured out the gift of the Holy Ghost. For they heard them speak with tongues, and magnify God. Then answered Peter, Can any man forbid water, that these should not be baptized, which have received the Holy Ghost as well as we? And he commanded them to be baptized in the name of the Lord. Then prayed they him to tarry certain days.*[2]

Acts 11:8-9: "But I said, 'Not so, Lord: For nothing common[3] *or unclean*[4] *has at any time entered into my mouth.' But the voice answered me again from heaven, 'What God has cleansed*[5] *that call not thou common*[6].'"*

Webster's New World Dictionary of the American Language defines common as: "1. belonging equally to or shared by every one or all. 2. belonging to the community at large, public, 3. of, from, by, or to all. 4. general, prevalent, widespread. 5. familiar, usual met with frequently. 6. ordinary, undistinguished. 7. having no rank."

Achan was a member of the Army of God under Joshua's leadership. He is an example of one who mishandled the uncommon thing and profaned it. God had declared Jericho clean and holy to Himself. Israel was to utterly destroy the whole city including its inhabitants except for Rahab's household (Joshua 6:16-19). Achan ignored the ban and kept some of the precious stones and metals for himself. He hid them in his tent where he thought no one would find them. When Israel failed to conquer Ai, Joshua confronted God for failing to deliver Ai into Israel's hands as God had promised (Joshua 7:6-9). It was then that Achan's secret became common knowledge to Israel. The Holy Spirit directed a search of the camp and brought the leaders to the tent of Achan. There He pointed out the very spot where Achan had placed the holy or sacred things he had removed from Jericho. For this sin of mishandling the holy things of God, Achan and his family died that day under the judgment of God.

Belshazzar's profaning of the holy vessels of God is another example (Dan. 5:2-16). Belshazzar ruled Babylon during his father's, Nabonidus, 10 year absence. The terms, "his father, Nebuchadnezzar" (v2) and "his son" (v22), affirms Nebuchadnezzar's continued dynasty. Belshazzar should have learned from his predecessor the grace of humility but did not. God judged him and found him lacking because he served his lords, his wives, and his concubines wine from the vessels that Nebuchadnezzar took from the temple in Jerusalem. As they drank, they praised the gods of gold and silver, bronze and iron, wood and stone. Then the fingers of a man's hand appeared and wrote a message on the wall of the palace. The king called Daniel to interpret the message. Daniel explained that it was the hand of the Most High God who wrote the message. The message declared that God had numbered Belshazzar's kingdom and it would end. The message stated that God had judged him to be deficient and therefore He would divide his kingdom among the Medes and Persians.

Whatever has received the anointing of God is therefore holy and it is dangerous to treat it as common. Attributing the works of the Holy Spirit to Satan (Matt. 12:31-32) is another example. David's refusal to touch King Saul, "the LORD's anointed"; even though the king was seeking to kill him is also an example of God's sanctified vessels being uncommon and not to be profaned (1 Sam. 24:10). Passing off the words of an individual to be God's words is equally dangerous i.e., "Thus saith the Lord" when God has not spoken. God's concern about the things he has proclaimed clean should serve as a warning of His concern about everything that is holy or clean. We are accountable to know how God feels about everything so as not to regard that which He has cleansed as common, unclean or profane (Isa. 5:20). This book will investigate some of the things one must never ever consider common or ordinary.

CHAPTER 1

YHWH

When God identified Himself to Moses by the name, "I Am Who I Am" (Exod. 3:14), He unveiled His character and His attributes. Moses' subsequent encounter with Pharaoh and the children of Israel was not a matter of who Moses was but Who was with Moses. The author is convinced that this knowledge of God and His character and its firm belief is the key to a believer's success and prosperity. J. B. Phillips was also convinced of this when he wrote the challenging book, *Your God Is Too Small*. The prophet, Daniel, predicted that when the king from the north will come "by smooth words he will turn to godlessness those who act wickedly toward the covenant, but the people who know their God will display strength and take action (NASU, Dan. 11:32)." Knowing God is what enables believers to stand firm in the face of adversity and all challenging situations.

"Jehovah" and "Yahweh" are the transliterations of this name for God. In most English Bible translations it is printed "LORD". The Hebrew word is obscure because the consonants are all that exist in the Hebrew text. This is because the Hebrew people never spoke this name because it is the personal name of God. Since it was never spoken there were no vowels from the oral usage to be added to the Masoretic text when it was converted from all consonants. This name (YHWH) is also combined with other words to form new names for God and thus further reveal His character and nature. To take on such a huge topic for such a short time as one hour or one day or one year or even one life-time is presumptuous. So to avoid entering into presumptuousness one can explore only briefly some of the attributes of the One who is all in all, and greater than the universe itself.

God is Righteous.

Many scriptures make it evident that God is righteous and His actions and judgments are righteous also. Because God is righteous He cannot do anything that is unrighteous. He is incapable of doing anything that is not according to His nature. "Now therefore stand still, that I may reason with you before the Lord of all the righteous acts of the Lord, which he did to you and to your fathers (1 Sam. 12:7)." "O Lord God of Israel, thou art righteous: for we remain yet escaped, as it is this day: behold, we are before thee in our trespasses: for we cannot stand before thee because of this (Ezra 9:15)." "For the righteous Lord loveth righteousness; his countenance doth behold the upright (Psa. 11:7)." "The fear of the Lord is clean, enduring forever: the judgments of the Lord are true and righteous altogether (Psa. 19:9)." "Gracious is the Lord, and righteous; yea, our God is merciful (Psa. 116:5)." "Righteous art thou, O Lord, and upright are thy judgments (Psa. 119:137)."

The word righteousness comes from a root Hebrew word (*tsâdaq*)[1] that means "to be right (in a moral or forensic sense); to clear oneself; to cleanse; to be straight, to be just, to be true, to be upright, to be righteous; to be in the right; to be justified, to obtain one's cause (in a forensic sense (Isa. 45:25)), to be restored, to be exonerated; to justify, to declare to be righteous; to make righteous, to declare someone innocent or righteous; to be vindicated from wrongs, to be exonerated; to absolve, to acquit, to approve of, to have a just cause."[2] Righteousness then refers to a state that conforms to an authoritative standard. Therefore righteousness is a moral expression. God's character consequently is the definition and source of all righteousness.

"'Peradventure there be fifty righteous within the city: wilt thou also destroy and not spare the place for the fifty righteous that are therein? That be far from thee to do after this manner, to slay the righteous with the wicked: and that the righteous should be as the wicked, that be far from thee: Shall not the Judge of all the earth do right?' And the Lord said, 'If I find in Sodom fifty righteous within the city, then I will spare all the place for their sakes' (Gen 18:24-26)." "The Lord is righteous in all his ways, and holy in all his works (Psa. 119:17)." "What shall we say then? Is there unrighteousness with God? God forbid (Rom. 9:14)." Because God is righteous it is impossible for Him to act unrighteous and we must never attribute unrighteous acts, thoughts or words to Him or from Him.

Man's Righteousness

Therefore, man's righteousness must be defined considering God's righteousness. Holy and upright living is living according to God's standard and not society or culture. Righteousness as applied to God refers to His affirmation of what is right as opposed to what is wrong. It refers to His moral laws laid down to guide the conduct of humankind, as in the Ten Commandments. It also refers to God's administration of justice. He brings punishment upon the disobedient (Rom. 2:1-16).

God's righteousness is redemptive.

In the Book of Romans the righteousness of God refers to God declaring the believer to be in a state of righteousness as though he had never been unrighteous. This is possible because of the sacrificial death of Jesus for mankind. "For I am not ashamed of the gospel of Christ: for it is the power of God unto salvation to everyone that believeth; to the Jew first, and also to the Greek. For therein is the righteousness of God revealed from faith to faith: as it is written, The just shall live by faith (Rom. 1:16-17)." "Being justified freely by his grace through the redemption that is in Christ Jesus: Whom God hath set forth to be a propitiation through faith in his blood, to declare his righteousness for the remission of sins that are past, through the forbearance of God; To declare, I say, at this time his righteousness: that he might be just, and the justifier of him which believeth in Jesus. Where is boasting then? It is excluded. By what law? of works? Nay: but by the law of faith. Therefore we conclude that a man is justified by faith without the deeds of the law (Rom. 3:24-28)."

In 2 Corinthians chapter five, Paul describes this righteousness of redeemed man: "Therefore if any man be in Christ, he is a new creature: old things are passed away; behold, all things are become new" (v17). He goes on to explain how it happened: "For he hath made him to be sin for us, who knew no sin; that we might be made the righteousness of God in him" (v21). For Righteous God to impute His righteousness to sinful man, it was necessary for righteous, sinless Jesus to take upon Himself the sinfulness of humanity and pay the just penalty required for this sin. Then Righteous God could declare redeemed man to be righteous.

God is also holy.

The words translated "holy" come from Greek and Hebrew root words that mean "to separate". It refers to moral and ethical wholeness or perfection; freedom from moral evil. It denotes that which is "sanctified" or "set apart" for divine service. Thus, it refers to God as separated from or exalted above other things.

15

"Who is like unto thee, O Lord, among the gods? Who is like thee, glorious in holiness, fearful in praises, doing wonders" (Ex. 15:11)? "All my bones shall say, Lord, who is like unto thee, which deliverest the poor from him that is too strong for him, yea, the poor and the needy from him that spoileth him" (Psa. 35:10)? "Thy righteousness also, O God, is very high, who hast done great things: O God, who is like unto thee" (Psa. 71:19)! "Who is like unto the Lord our God, who dwelleth on high," (Psa. 113:5). "Behold, he shall come up like a lion from the swelling of Jordan against the habitation of the strong: but I will suddenly make him run away from her: and who is a chosen man, that I may appoint over her? for who is like me? and who will appoint me the time? and who is that shepherd that will stand before me" (Jer. 49:19)? "Behold, he shall come up like a lion from the swelling of Jordan unto the habitation of the strong: but I will make them suddenly run away from her: and who is a chosen man, that I may appoint over her? for who is like me? and who will appoint me the time? and who is that shepherd that will stand before me" (Jer. 50:44)? "And they worshipped the dragon which gave power unto the beast: and they worshipped the beast, saying, Who is like unto the beast? who is able to make war with him" (Rev. 13:4)? "In the year that king Uzziah died I saw also the Lord sitting upon a throne, high and lifted up, and his train filled the temple. Above it stood the seraphims: each one had six wings; with twain he covered his face, and with twain he covered his feet, and with twain he did fly. And one cried unto another, and said, Holy, holy, holy, is the Lord of hosts: the whole earth is full of his glory" (Isa. 6:1-3).

Holiness refers to God's moral excellence. Sanctification and godliness are also renderings of these Hebrew and Greek words. Holiness is one of the essential elements of God's nature required of His people. Because God is holy, He demands holiness in His own children. What He demands, He also supplies. Holiness is God's gift received by faith through His Son, Jesus Christ. "And that ye put on the new man, which after God is created in righteousness and true holiness" (Eph. 4:24). God instructed Moses to "consecrate Aaron and his sons" to the priesthood (Ex 29:9). Moses admonished the children of Israel to "remember the Sabbath day and to keep it holy." The "Holy of Holies" was the most sacred place in the tabernacle and in the Temple at Jerusalem. Elisha was known as a "holy man of God." Herod feared John the Baptist, "Knowing that he was a just and holy man" (Mark 6:20).

The main use of holy is to describe God's righteous nature or the ethical righteousness demanded of and exemplified in His followers. Holiness is a unique quality of His character. The Bible emphasizes this divine attribute. "Who is like you, O Lord" (Ex. 15:11)? "There is none holy like the Lord" (1Sam. 2:2). "Who shall not fear You, O Lord . . . For You alone are holy"

(Rev. 15:4). God's high expectations of His people flow out of His own holy nature: "You shall be to me a kingdom of priests and a holy nation" (Ex. 19:6); "sanctify yourselves therefore and be holy, for I am the Lord your God" (Lev. 20:7). Since He is the Holy One Himself, He makes all other holy things holy and all other uncommon things uncommon.

Jesus as the incarnate Son of God was the personification of holiness. He reiterated God's demands for holiness by insisting that His disciples must have a higher quality of righteousness than that of the scribes and Pharisees (Matt. 5:20). He was not willing to accept ceremonial holiness: "I desire mercy and not sacrifice" (Matt. 12:7). He was not willing to accept self-righteousness but demanded Godly righteousness. Without this righteousness the disciples would not enter the kingdom of heaven. Jesus thus defined the legalism and hypocrisy of the Pharisees and scribes as common. This righteousness is not earned or the result of good works but imputed to believers through the sacrificial death of Jesus.

The theme of sanctification, or maturing into God's likeness and being set apart for His use was a distinct message of the apostles. They taught that patient, loving service while awaiting the Lord's return is the expression of sanctification, or true holiness. Peter urged the suffering believers to follow God's example of holiness in their trials: "As He who has called you is holy, you also be holy in all your conduct because it is written 'Be holy, for I am holy'" (1Pet. 1:15)!

Paul prayed for the believers at Thessalonica: "And may the Lord make you increase in love and abound in love to one another and to all, just as we do to you so that He may establish your hearts blameless in holiness before our God and Father at the coming of our Lord Jesus Christ with all His saints" (1Thes. 3:12-13). It has timeless application for all saints. When one settles for less he is treating the sanctifying work of God as ordinary, or common. He is living before a holy God as though He were merely his equal. To fail to repent of sin is to consider the righteousness of God as cheap and profane viewing the redemptive work of Jesus as normal or common.

God is just.

His judgments are always right and true. "And I heard another out of the altar say, Even so, Lord God Almighty, true and righteous are thy judgments" (Rev. 16:7). "The fear of the Lord is clean, enduring forever: the judgments of the Lord are true and righteous altogether" (Psa. 19:9). God always treats people justly. He follows His commandments as well as that which makes for reconciliation with Him and among individuals. Biblical justice exceeds the law courts and legal justice by including everyday life. When husbands and wives, parents and children, employers and employees, government and citizens, and human being and God maintain honorable relationships, justice is done. Justice refers to brotherliness in spirit and action. God requires that believers "do justly and love mercy and walk humbly with your God" (Micah 6:8). His emphasis is "doing" rather than the human emphasis of "getting". One must not only see that he does right but seek to make things right that are wrong in order to fulfill justice's demand. The modern idea of who wins the case without regard for whether the person is guilty or innocent is less than godly justice. To allow a guilty person to go free because of some "legal" technicality seems to profane real justice. It seems to put more emphasis on the method than what is right or just.

In the Hebrew there is a root connection between righteousness, justice and judgment. God so linked these words so that one depends upon the others. One is not possible without the others. God ordained governments to maintain justice and righteousness in nations (Rom. 13:1-14). He empowered them to give justice (Biblical justice) to each citizen and visitor. This means that government officials are ministers of God even as pastors. To exercise one's responsibilities unjustly is to treat God as common or ordinary. To "plea bargain" for expedience may be good legal practice but it is disrespectful for the one who ordained justice. If the dockets are too full then get more judges as Moses was instructed to do. If the crimes committed are so many, then repentance is more important than ever. Kings, rulers, and those in power are to be instruments of justice (Psa. 72:1), as exemplified by David and Josiah. Isaiah describes the suffering servant, messiah, as one whose task as ruler will be to bring justice to the nations (Isa. 42:1-4). Jesus of Nazareth is the fulfillment of that prophecy.

The prophets of the Old Testament were the champions of social justice when bribery and inequity often perverted justice. God, however, rewards those who practice justice in all their dealings with others. God deals fairly and impartially with all people. As a God of justice, He is interested in fairness as well as in what makes for right relationships. His actions and decisions are true and right (Rev. 16:7). He demands that individuals and nations look after victims of oppression (Psa. 82). The Lord and Judge of the earth brings justice to nations and sets things right on behalf of the poor, the oppressed, and the victims of injustice. The Supreme Judge of the earth brings justice to the wicked, the unjust, and the oppressor. God's just action is reason for hope for all who are unjustly treated. "Little children, let no man deceive you: he that doeth righteousness is righteous, even as He is righteous" (1John 3:7). Job was questioned by God about his judging the justice of God (Job 40:8).

God is Sovereign.

Many have often misused and misunderstood this term. Much of the earlier part of this chapter speaks to this aspect of Almighty God. God is the creator and sustainer of the universe who has provided humankind with a revelation of Himself through the natural world (Psa. 19:1; Rom. 1:19-20) and through His Son, Jesus Christ.

Sovereign is a theological term that refers to the unlimited power of God, who has sovereign control over the affairs of nature and history. The Old Testament sees all of life as God's responsibility therefore it reports the stubbornness of Pharaoh as God's hardening of his heart. This aspect of God's nature must be understood in the context of all of His divine nature. The Bible declares that God is working out His sovereign plan of redemption for the world and that the conclusion is certain. To infer that this sovereignty makes God the cause of everything that happens, however, is to profane Him to a level less than moral man. Immediately after the fall of Adam, God declared the curse of human sin and illustrated its cure. To the serpent He said, "I will put enmity between you and the woman, and between your seed and her seed; He shall bruise your head, and you shall bruise His heel" (Gen. 3:15). Hence the whole redemptive story of the Bible is the fulfillment of this prophecy by the sovereign God. God's sovereignty did not demand that His Son come to earth and die. This was negotiated before the earth was ever formed.

From Genesis to Revelation the redemption story demonstrates the love the sovereign God has for the created world, fallen though it is, and His ability to do something about it. Without the benevolent love of the Father spread abroad in the believer's heart by the Holy Spirit and the selfless sacrifice of Jesus, the Son, there would be no freedom from sin nor any hope of eternal life.

God used King Nebuchadnezzar to bring judgment upon sinful Israel. His sinful treatment of innocent people and disregard for God's sovereignty brought God's judgment upon him. He tried to burn three righteous Hebrew boys who refused to become spiritual adulators by bowing to his image of gold. God warned him in a dream which Daniel interpreted by God's Spirit. Sovereign God's kingship challenged Nebuchadnezzar's pride. In his humbling experience of eating grass like the cattle, Nebuchadnezzar recognized the Most High God as king of heaven and earth. This encounter did not leave him arrogant or angry at God but brought him to praise and bless and honor the King of Heaven (Dan. 4:34-37).

God is changeless.

Progress and change may characterize some of His works, but God Himself remains unchanged (Heb. 1:12). If He were to change it would mean that He is not perfect. Thus, what one knows of God he knows with certainty. He is not different from one moment or age to another (Mal 3:6). The God of the Old Testament is the God of the New Testament. God's attitude toward sinful humanity has not changed. Because of Jesus' future death on the cross God showed mercy to the Old Testament people by postponing judgment until Jesus satisfied justice's demand. When someone questions whether justice will find the evil doers of this day who apparently are getting by with their evil, he has forgotten that God does not change. Therefore, God's words are as true today as they were when they were spoken or written.

God Is All Powerful.

His power is unlimited (Gen 18:14). Nevertheless He cannot do anything that is inconsistent with His nature, character, or purpose (Gen 18:25). The only limitations on God's power are Self-imposed. "Impossible" is not even in His vocabulary. God creates and sustains all things; yet He never grows weary (Isa. 40:27-31).

Omnipotence is a theological word that refers to the all-encompassing power of God. The Almighty God expects human beings to obey Him, and He holds them responsible for their thoughts and actions. Nevertheless, He is the all-powerful Lord who has created all things and sustains them by the Word of His power. "In the beginning God created the heaven and the earth. And the earth was without form, and void; and darkness was upon the face of the deep. And the Spirit of God moved upon the face of the waters. And God said, 'Let there be light': and there was light" (Gen. 1:1-3). "Who being the brightness of his glory, and the express image of his person, and upholding all things by the word of his power, when he had by himself purged our sins, sat down on the right hand of the Majesty on high" (Heb. 1:3). "Behold, the nations are as a drop of a bucket, and are counted as the small dust of the balance: behold, he taketh up the isles as a very little thing" (Isa. 40:15). Have you ever laid on your back and looked up at the sky at night and watched the stars. It is hard to imagine that the light we see left that star years ago and is just now reaching us. Sirius, one of the brightest stars, is 8.6 light years away. Light travels at 700 million miles per hour or 6 quadrillion miles per year. That means Sirius is about 52 quadrillion miles away from earth. God created this universe and keeps it going. He is the one who covenants to always be with us. When we pray and still allow our circumstances to cast us into hopeless despair are we not questioning God's power? Are we not acting like the Children of Israel as they visited the promised-land and saw themselves as grasshoppers before the giants of the land? They had a Word from God promising His gift of the land but they reasoned that they couldn't possess the land held by these giants with their walled cities because God wasn't powerful enough to keep His promise.

God Is All Knowing.

God possesses all knowledge and wisdom (Rom. 11:33-36). Because God is everywhere at the same time, He knows everything simultaneously. Omniscience is the theological term that refers to God's superior knowledge and wisdom, His ability to know all things. God is the Lord who knows man's thoughts from afar. He is knowledgeable of all man's ways, knowing his words even before they are on his tongue. God in His wisdom knows the thoughts and motives of every heart (Isa.40:28 and Rom. 11:33). David writes:

> "O Lord, thou hast searched me, and known me. Thou knowest my downsitting and mine uprising, thou understandest my thought afar off. Thou compassest my path and my lying down, and art acquainted with all my ways. For there is not a word in my tongue, but, lo, O Lord, thou knowest it altogether. Thou hast beset me behind and before, and laid thine hand upon me. Such knowledge is too wonderful for me; it is high, I cannot attain unto it. For thou hast possessed my reins: thou hast covered me in my mother's womb. I will praise thee; for I am fearfully and wonderfully made: marvellous are thy works; and that my soul knoweth right well. My substance was not hid from thee, when I was made in secret, and curiously wrought in the lowest parts of the earth. Thine eyes did see my substance, yet being unperfected; and in thy book all my members were written, which in continuance were fashioned, when as yet there was none of them" (Psa. 139:1-6, 13-16).

He does not need to consult any one for knowledge or understanding (Isa. 40:13-14). He is the all-knowing Lord who prophesies the events of the future, including the death of His Son (Isa. 53) and the return of Christ at the end of this age when death will be finally overcome (Rom. 8:18-39; 1 Cor. 15:51-57). Only a God who is all-knowing and all-powerful can perform a change in believers during the present age that will guarantee freedom from sin, decay, and death in eternity. To live one's life as though God is ignorant of one's affairs is to profane the Omniscient One. To believe that we can hide anything from Him, is to consider Him to be only human.

God is always present everywhere.

God is present in all His power at every point in space and time therefore no part of the universe or any country is outside His realm (Ps. 139:7-12). Omnipresence is the theological term that refers to the unlimited nature of God or His ability to be always everywhere. God is not like the manufactured idols that are limited to one altar or temple area or wherever His worshipers might carry Him. God reveals Himself in the Bible as the Lord who is everywhere. God was present as Lord in all creation (Psa. 139:13-16) and there is no escaping Him. He is present in one's innermost thoughts. Even as one is being formed in the womb, He knows all the days of his future. God sees in secret and rewards in secret, as Jesus taught His disciples; He looks not only on outward actions, but especially on the inner attitudes of a person's heart (Matt. 6:1-18). Because God is the creator and sustainer of time and space, He is everywhere. Being everywhere, He is the great Comforter, Friend, and Redeemer. Thus, God does not belong to any one nation or generation. He is the God of all the earth (Gen. 18:25). To believe that He confines Him to one nation or people is to make Him common or ordinary. Jonah's sin is an example of this. He thought he could run from God but learned an important lesson for all. He also learned that God's infinite love was also for sinful Nineveh. One repeats Jonah's sin when he thinks that God does not care about the homosexual, alcoholic, drug addict, prostitute, Muslim, Communist, or any other human being.

God Is Eternal.

Eternity refers to God's relationship to time. He knows equally past, present, and future. He is, He was, and He shall always be (2 Pet. 3:8; Rev. 1:8; 16:5). Time is like a long freight train that man sees only a portion at a time but God sees its entirety. The Bible never seeks to prove God's existence. Its opening words simply set God as being present when everything begins, "In the beginning God created." The Hebrew word "beginning" is plural, "beginnings" and emphasizes that God has always been.

God is a Father.

Jesus refers to God as His Father with whom He is equal. Jesus also taught His disciples to address God as Father and warns against calling anyone else Father. Throughout the Scriptures there are many teachings concerning fatherhood. God, our Heavenly Father, is the perfection of these teachings. All that the Bible exhorts an earthly father to do for his family and children, God does for His family and children. To accuse God of doing anything an earthly father would not do is to profane or make common our Heavenly Father. Jesus teaches in the Sermon on the Mount the futility of trying to serve two masters or gods (Matt. 6:22-34). One must decide whom he will serve. Jesus then illustrates this truth by speaking of anxiety or worry. To worry about what the Father provides is the same as idolatry or serving another God. It makes our Heavenly Father a common god. It turns one's attention away from El Shaddai (The All Sufficient One) to things or circumstances. Jesus then shows how futile and unsuccessful this is. He asks some probing questions about the benefits of worry. James and Peter both emphasize the need for humility as the answer (Jas. 4:1-10; 1Pet. 5:5-9). Praise is one of the ways to do this. Praise focuses one's attention on a Holy God who is our Father. It recognizes the greatness of God and one's dependence on Him for everything. Humility takes the citation out of one's hands and puts it in God's.

The conclusion

The conclusion then is that God is Holy and to call Him anything else is to profane what is clean. God therefore deserves to be Lord of one's life. Sometimes one strikes out against the callings of God and seeks his own end. This person doubts that God really knows best or can sustain him in all circumstances. There is a day in the life of every person when he comes face to face with the Great I Am. Saul on the Damascus Road is an example. God deserves to be in charge of your life. He can do it better than you. Surrender control of your life to Jesus and the Holy Spirit. While working as a computer programmer in the space industry, the author was faced with God's call to resign his position and move to another city and enter seminary. It was a challenge to trust God to care for his family and provide for his schooling. Government grants were not yet conceived and he had college loans to repay. The author and his wife prayed together and decided to follow God direction. At this writing that was forty-seven years ago and they have no regrets. James, the brother of Jesus, warns against making plans without consulting God. To do so is to brag of what one does not possess. It is pompous pride that would presume that one is in charge of his life and this world (Jas. 4: 13-14). If one lives for Him and with Him, his life will have merit. God's peace and love will come. All the fruit of the Spirit will come. No amount of pleading or begging will be sufficient, only complete surrender. True freedom is experienced only when one submits fully to the Lord. One cannot move on to maturity until he takes the basic step of honoring God as clean and holy. This step is continual like taking up one's cross daily. One cannot think as God thinks (theologically) until he recognizes that God is not common. One must not call unclean or common that which is holy and clean.

CHAPTER 2

"HALLOWED BE THY NAME"[1]

The various names given to God in the Bible serve to indicate man's understanding of God and His attributes. The priests were set aside to make the name of God known among the people. Their task was to keep the name of the Lord holy and not to profane it. "They shall be holy unto their God, and not profane the name of their God: for the offerings of the Lord made by fire, and the bread of their God, they do offer: therefore they shall be holy (Lev. 21:6)." "Speak unto Aaron and to his sons, that they separate themselves from the holy things of the children of Israel, and that they profane not my holy name in those things which they hallow unto me: I am the Lord (Lev. 22:2)." "Neither shall ye profane my holy name; but I will be hallowed among the children of Israel: I am the Lord which hallow you (Lev. 22:32)."

A name is a label or designation that sets one person apart from another. In the Bible a name is much more than an identifier as it tends to be in American culture. Personal names and names of places were formed from words that had their own meaning. Thus, the people of the Bible were very conscious of the meaning of names. They believed there was a vital connection between the name and the person it identified. A name somehow represented the nature of the person. This means that the naming of a baby was very important in the Bible. In choosing a name, the parents could reflect the circumstances of the child's birth, their own feelings, their gratitude to God, their hopes and prayers for the child, and their commitment of the child to God. For example, the name Isaac reflected the "laughter" of his mother at his birth (Gen. 21:6). Esau was named "hairy" because of his appearance. Jacob was named "supplanter" because he grasped his brother, Esau's, heel

Gen. 25:25-26). Moses received his name because he was "drawn out" of the water.

A popular custom of Bible times was to compose names by using the shortened forms of the divine name *El* or *Ya* (Je) as the beginning or ending syllable. Examples of this practice are: Elisha, "God is salvation"; Daniel, "God is my judge"; Jehoiakim, "the Lord has established"; and Isaiah, "the Lord is salvation." Sometimes very specialized names, directly related to circumstances of the parents, were given to children. The prophet Isaiah was directed to name one of his children *Maher-Shalal-Hash-Baz*, "speed the spoil, hasten the prey." This name was an allusion to the certain Assyrian invasion of the nation of Judah (Isa. 8:3-4). Hosea was instructed to name a daughter *Lo-Ruhamah*, "no mercy," and a son Lo-Ammi, "not my people." Both of these names referred to God's displeasure with His people, Israel (Hos. 1:6-9).

The change of a name can also be of great importance in the Bible. Abram's name was changed to Abraham in connection with his new calling to be "a father of many nations" (Gen. 17:5). God gave Jacob the new name, Israel, "God strives," because he "struggled with God and with men, and prevailed (Gen. 32:28; 35:10)."

In the giving or taking of new names, often a crucial turning point in the person's life has been reached. Simon was given the name Peter, "stone or little rock," because he was to be foundational in the forming of the church that Christ would build (Matt. 16:18). Saul was renamed Paul, a Greek name that was appropriate for one who was destined to become the great apostle to the Gentiles.

The connection between a name and the reality it signified is nowhere more important than in the names referring to God. The personal name of God revealed to Moses in the burning bush, "I AM WHO I AM," (Exod. 3:14) conveyed something of His character. The name of the Lord (Jehovah-*Shammah*) was virtually synonymous with His presence: "For your wondrous works declare that your name is near (Psa. 75:1)." To know the name of God is thus to know God Himself. For this reason, to "take the name of the Lord your God in vain (Exod. 20:7)" is to act in any way that is inconsistent with the profession that He is the Lord God.

The New Testament writers also emphasized the importance of names and the close relationship between names and what they mean. A striking illustration of this is: "For there is no other name under heaven by which we must be saved (Acts 4:12)." In this instance the name is again practically interchangeable with the reality which it represents. Christians were described by the apostle Paul as those who "name the name of the Lord (2 Tim. 2:19)." A true understanding of the exalted Jesus is often connected with a statement about His name. Thus, Jesus "has by inheritance obtained a more excellent name" than the angels (Heb. 1:4), and "God also has highly exalted Him and given Him the name which is above every name (Phil. 2:9)."

An important root name for God in the Old Testament is *El*. It is a general reference to a god. It was widely used in ancient eastern cultures whose languages are similar to Hebrew and therefore may refer either to the true God or to false gods. The highest Canaanite god was *El* whose son was Baal. To distinguish the One True God, the Bible uses qualifiers. An example is: ". . . I, the LORD (*YHWH*) your God (*Elohim*), am a jealous God (*El*) . . ."(Deut. 5:9). Another example is: "And when Abraham was ninety years old and nine, the LORD (*YHWH*) appeared to Abram, and said unto him 'I am the Almighty (*Shadday*) God (*El*); walk before me, and be thou perfect (Gen. 17:1).'"Throughout Israel's history she has profaned the name of God by seeing Him as another of the gods. Today there are some who speak of many ways to god. They think that *Allah, Shiva,* or *Vishnu* are as much god as God. Some say there is only one God but many names according to culture and nation. The Bible disagrees and calls such ideas a profaning of the name of God.

Elohiym

Elohiym is the plural form of *El*, but it is usually translated in the singular. Some scholars have held that the plural represents an intensified form for the supreme God since other eastern languages used the plural form to identify deity; others believe it describes the supreme God and His heavenly court of created beings such as angels and the heavenly court of judgment or Israel's council of Elders (judges) (Psa. 82). Still others hold that the plural form refers to the triune God of Genesis 1:1-3, who works through Word and Spirit in the creation of the world. This view opens Christianity to the Islamic allegation that Christianity is polytheistic. Trinity does not mean three gods. It is no more plural than "man" who is tripartite or a dichotomy. All agree that the plural form *Elohiym* does convey the sense of the "one supreme being" who is the only true God.

El Shaddai

El Shaddai[2] (God Almighty), signifying God as a source of blessing, is the name with which God appeared to Abraham, Isaac, and Jacob (Exod. 6:3). This means that until Moses the covenant name of God was *El Shaddai*. He showed Himself to be the God of "more than enough." The Rabbis believed that the name meant the "One who is self-sufficient." This name identifies

Him as the "Breasted One" and therefore the source. This name also sets God apart from all other gods. The Septuagint has *pantokratwr* (*pantokrator*) which indicates the "One Who Rules" or "Almighty" or "Omnipotent". He is the One for whom nothing is impossible. To forget this is to call Almighty God common or ordinary.

Yahweh

One of the most important names for God in the Old Testament is Yahweh, or Jehovah, from the Hebrew verb "to be," meaning simply but profoundly, "I am who I am," and "I will be who I will be." The four-letter Hebrew word *YHWH* (YHWH))) was the name by which God revealed Himself to Moses in the burning bush (Exod. 3:14). The divine name, Yahweh, is usually translated, LORD, in English versions of the Bible, because it became a practice in late Old Testament Judaism not to pronounce the sacred name *YHWH*, but to say instead "my Lord" (*Adonai*)—a practice still used today in the synagogue. When the vowels of *Adonai* were attached to the consonants *YHWH* in the Masoretic text, the word "Jehovah" resulted. Today, many Christians use the word Yahweh, the more original pronunciation, not hesitating to name the divine name since Jesus taught believers to speak in a familiar way to God. Some English translations of the Bible translate the word as Jehovah, while others use *Yahweh*.

From Moses onward this was the covenant name for God. He is the author of life and salvation. This name best expresses that. It was combined with other names to express the fact that He is the infinite and original personal God who is behind everything and to whom everything must finally be traced. This name reminds one that nothing else defines who God is but God Himself, "I am who I am." His nature is expressed in all He does and says. In the Bible God defines Himself by what He says about Himself and what He does. *Yahweh* is the all-powerful and sovereign God who alone defines Himself and establishes truth for His creatures and works for their salvation. In the deliverance of the Hebrew people from slavery in Egypt, God revealed a deeper significance to His name. He had already disclosed Himself to Abraham, Isaac, and Jacob as *Yahweh*. Each of them had called on the name of the Lord, *Yahweh*,[3] as the God who protects and blesses. However, Exodus 6:3 declares that they did not "know" Him by that name. This seeming contradiction is explainable in light of the word translated "known"[4]. The meaning of this word is "to know by instruction or observation." Hence God was declaring that Israel was about to observe a greater demonstration of *Yahweh* than had previously been experienced. The exodus from Egypt was a demonstration of the power of God unknown to Abraham, Isaac, and Jacob. Moses was called upon to proclaim deliverance to the people by the hand of "I Am"

The following are names that are built on the stem from the basic name of *Yahweh*. They illustrate the several ways God revealed Himself to His people:

Jehovah-Jireh

Jehovah-Jireh is translated as "The-Lord-Will-Provide." It commemorates God's provision of the ram in place of Isaac for Abraham's sacrifice (Gen. 22:14). Its significance is wrapped up in the knowledge that He is *El Shaddai* who is "more than enough." This is the name Paul had in mind when he told the church in Philippi "my God will supply all your needs according to His riches in glory in Christ Jesus (NASU, Phil 4:19)."

Jehovah-Nissi

Jehovah-Nissi, "The-Lord-Is-My-Banner," is in honor of God's defeat of the Amalekites (Ex. 17:15). Isaiah says the enemy comes in like a flood but the Lord will lift up a standard (banner) against him (Isa. 59:19). This is a military term referring to the banner or flag that flies over the people of God. When one lives and behaves like the unbelieving world he defiles the banner that flies over him. Wherever he goes he should be conscious that the banner goes with him and it can be profaned by the place to which he goes and his actions.

Jehovah-Rohi

This phrase translates, "The-Lord-Is-Shepherd (Psa. 23:1; John 10:11-18)." God as one's shepherd provides for his maturing and growing-up. He has purposed that the believer be conformed to the expressed image of His Son (Rom. 8:29). As the shepherd He provides good pasture (feeding places) and good water to drink (Holy Spirit) and leads him in the paths of righteousness. The Lord will love him and care for him as a good shepherd. He carries him when he is weak or injured. He fights the bear and the lion for him and prevents them from devouring him. Solomon writes, "The name of the Lord is a strong tower, the righteous run into it and are safe (Prov. 18:10)." He must have learned this from his father, who wrote Psalms 91. David had learned that the one who was his shepherd was the all sufficient, *El Shaddai*. Everyone needs to know this also. To act as though their helper or shepherd of their souls is not able to help them is to defile the name of the Lord the Shepherd.

Jehovah-Raphá

This phrase translates, "The-Lord-Is-Healer," the name Moses used as Israel leaves Egypt (Exod. 15:26). It is God who brings health to His people. Israel was kept healthy throughout the wilderness wanderings. The snake bites were rendered ineffective to those that looked at the staff provided by the Lord. Those who looked received. Since God does not change He is still the healer of His people. His healing provision is for all that man is. Isaiah prophesied that the messiah would carry the sicknesses and diseases of those for whom He died (Isa. 53:4, 5). Peter reminds everyone that it is "by His stripes that we were healed (1 Pet. 2:24)." To deny the healing power of God toward one is to profane the name of the Lord the Healer. To not look to Him for healing is to ignore the name with healing within it.

Jehovah-Shalom

This phrase means "The-Lord-Is-Peace," the name Gideon gave the altar that he built in Ophrah (Judg. 6:24). Even when the odds are overwhelming, God gives one peace. When one becomes anxious and restless he profanes the God who is his peace. Jesus says that one cannot serve two masters. Anxiousness and worry reflect that one is trying to serve two and Jehovah-Shalom is profaned. The author learned this lesson while experiencing a hurricane. The eye had settled over the island for three days. While eating lunch on the third day he realized that he had a stress headache. The realization brought peace and God caused the hurricane to just disappear off the radar. The temporary peace of the eye was replaced with the Peace of God.

Jehovah-Shammah

This phrase expresses the truth that "The-Lord-Is-There," referring to the city which the prophet Ezekiel saw in his vision (Ezek. 48:35). God is present no matter where one is or what is happening around him. This name is a reminder that God is omnipresent. When one runs like Jonah or acts as if God doesn't care, he fails to exemplify that God is there and thereby profane His name. Anyone who feels like God has taken a vacation only needs to turn around to discover that He is right there.

Jehovah-Tsebaoth

This name, translated "The-Lord-of-hosts," was used in the days of David and the prophets, to witness to God the Savior who is surrounded by His hosts of heavenly power (1Sam 1:3). When one is in trouble the God of hosts is on his side. Peter forgot this as he swung his sword at the servant. Fortunately he was a poor swordsman and missed, cutting off the man's ear. Jesus replaced it reminding Peter that the Lord of Hosts was present to assist Him. He didn't need a human fisherman, would-be swordsman. Peter had profaned the name of the Lord of Hosts. When one seeks to do it himself, his way, he also makes God common.

Jehovah Elohiym Israel[5]

This name means "Lord-God-of-Israel," and it appears in Exodus, the historical books and Isaiah, Jeremiah, and the Psalms. Other names similar to this are *Netsah Israel*, "The Strength of Israel (1Sam. 15:29)" and *Abir Yisrael*, "The Mighty One of Israel (Isa. 1:24)."

Yahweh Èl Elohiym[6]

This phrase means "Jehovah God of gods." It is used by Joshua to indicate that there are no other gods to compare with the Lord. To entertain the idea that any so-called god is anything but stone or wood or metal is to profane the Lord. There is only one God. Allah is not the Lord. Buddha is not God. You are not God. Krishna is not God. Satan is not God. Only the LORD is God.

The coming messiah was called by many names that expressed His nature and mission. These will be further discussed in another chapter. These names are: Branch of righteousness, King, Shepherd, Servant, and Word of God.

Jesus gave to the church His Name to use in prayer and warfare. This name is above every other name (Phil. 2:9). This name is to be used in casting out demons or evil spirits, speaking in tongues, take up serpents, drink deadly things, lay hands on the sick (Mark 16:15-19). Since the original Greek text does not contain punctuation verse seventeen could be translated: "And these signs will follow those who believe in My name: They will cast out demons; they will speak in new tongues." The power of this name and uses of it by the apostles and New Testament church is found in the book of Acts and the Epistles. Using the name of Jesus to handle poisonous snakes or drinking of poison or eating poisonous food in a religious ceremony is to take the name "in vain." Jesus was tempted of the Devil to do a similar thing in the temptation in the wilderness (Lk. 4:9-12; Matt. 4:5-7). Jesus said this was putting God to the test. Paul however was bitten by an asp on Malta (Acts 28:1-9). The natives expected him to die but he shook it off into the fire. The natives then decided that he must be a god and started to worship him. Paul then went to Publius'[7] house where his father was sick of a fever and dysentery. Paul laid his hands on him and he was healed. Likewise the other sick and diseased of the island came to Paul and were also healed. The first mentioned use of the name of Jesus by the New Testament Church records the healing of a lame man (Acts 3:1-22). The lame man was over forty years old and renowned for begging at the Beautiful Gate. His lameness was from birth. This use of the name of Jesus upset the Jews and they forbid the use of it by Peter and John. They were not agitated because the man was healed but because the name, Jesus of Nazareth, was used. The Jews did not mention the name of a dead person. Peter and John's use of the name maintained that Jesus was alive and not dead. One's use of the name today continues to proclaim that He is living. The Jews sought to profane the name of Jesus by forbidding its use. One can also profane the name of Jesus by not using it. Restricting its use or not allowing its use in healing or deliverance profanes it. Saying that God does not heal today or only on occasion is to make the name that is above every name common. Denying the existence of evil spirits or demons is to say that God's Word is not true and takes away from the power of the name.

Using the name as a profanity desecrates the mighty name of the Son of God and risks the wrath of God. The indiscriminate use of the name whether in vows, religious recitations, habitual expressions (i.e., "Praise the Lord") or pious speech is similarly irreverent. Using His name to authenticate one's opinions or desires (i.e., "The Lord said" or "Thus saith the Lord") is to profane the name. The commandment not to "take the name of the Lord thy God in vain (Exod. 20:7)" is still in effect. One must learn to restrain his tongue and bear in mind that God's name is inseparable from His personality. Jesus' name is likewise inseparable from His character. Asking for anything in the name of Jesus that is not compatible with His character is profanity. Behaving in a manner inconsistent with the nature of Christ and calling ourselves Christian is defiling the name of Jesus. Bumper stickers that identifies one as Christ-like (Christian) on cars that violate the principles of Christ's character is disrespectful.

Every believer has been given a great privilege to bear His name but with it also comes a greater accountability. Likewise, he has been commissioned with His name to use in prayer and warfare. "To whom much has been given will much be required (Lk. 12:28)." His Name is made common or ordinary when one is not trustworthy. Perhaps he needs to join the Apostles in their prayer for boldness: "grant unto thy servants that with all boldness they may speak thy word, by stretching forth thine hand to heal; and that signs and wonders may be done by the name of thy holy child Jesus (Acts 4:29-30)." Perhaps he needs to listen to the judgment upon Israel, God's People, as recorded in Ezekiel 36:20-38. When one is identified with the Name of God and fails to cause others to reverence it, he has profaned the Name of the Lord. Spiritual adultery (idolatry) is one way this is done. God intended for Israel to prosper and be an example to the heathen world. Her failure brought God's judgment in the form of captivities by the heathen. God's deliverance was an act of restoration not of Israel but the Name of the Lord (V22). Consulting fortune-tellers, clairvoyants, seers, mediums, palm readers, horoscopes, or ungodly counselors (wisdom of men) for guidance profanes the name of the Lord. To live one's life as though He only exists for worship on Sunday, or some other day, is to practice practical atheism and pollutes God's holy name. Unjust legal practices in a nation considered by the world to be Christian is to profane the Name of the Lord. Even worse is injustice within the church in its discipline and in its member's business dealings. God who is just has His name profaned when His people act unjustly. God is so committed to the maintaining of the excellence of His name that it is prophesied that at the close of this age He will again sanctify His name in all the earth and among all the peoples of the world (Ezek. 39:7). The great final victory over Gog and Magog is meant to accomplish this.

CHAPTER 3

JESUS CHRIST

Jesus means "Jehovah is Salvation," and is the equivalent of the Hebrew name, Joshua. There are five men so named in the New Testament. They are: 1. Jesus Barabbas, a prisoner released by the Roman governor Pontius Pilate before Jesus was crucified; 2. An ancestor of Christ; 3. The KJV rendering of Joshua, the son of Nun; 4. Jesus Justus, a Jewish Christian who, with the apostle Paul, sent greetings to the Colossians; 5. Jesus, the incarnate Son of God; born of the Virgin Mary; founder of the Christian church; the great High Priest who intercedes for His people at the right hand of God; and perfect man.

The twofold designation Jesus Christ combines the personal name Jesus and the title Christ, meaning "anointed one" or "Messiah." Christ showed that He was the long-awaited king and deliverer of Israel and mankind. For centuries the Jewish people had looked for a prophesied Messiah, a deliverer who would usher in a kingdom of peace and prosperity.[1] Peter's great confession, "Thou art the Christ, the Son of the living God" (Matt. 16:16) clearly identified Jesus as the Messiah. Jesus' teachings also declared that He was the Messiah.

Jesus was born in Bethlehem near the end of Herod the Great's reign as king of the Jews (37-4 B.C.). Bethlehem is a small village of about 300 inhabitants six miles south of Jerusalem. Early in His life after an escape journey to Egypt His family moved to the Galilean village of Nazareth. There He was brought up by His mother, Mary, and her husband, Joseph, a carpenter by trade. Hence He was known as "Jesus of Nazareth" or, more completely, "Jesus of Nazareth, the son of Joseph (John 1:45)." Being born of a virgin obviously means that Joseph was not His biological father. The Bible describes what happened to Mary in such a way as to rule out any sexual contact with a human male or spiritual being, even God. The expression that the Holy Spirit came upon her and the power of the Highest overshadowed her is far from an expression of sexual involvement (Luke 1:26-35; Matt. 1:18-20). The Holy Spirit simply placed the Logos into Mary's womb as a present day doctor might transplant a test tube embryo into a woman's womb. In Mary's womb the Logos became flesh. This would mean that Jesus was not even the biological son of Mary carrying her genes and heritage of sin. The word begotten is used in Matthew to describe this transaction. The word translated "overshadow" in Luke is the same as the one used concerning the transfiguration experience near the end of Jesus ministry (Matt. 17:5; Luke 1:35). Hence it does not indicate sexual contact. What took place with Mary was not common. It was a unique event which produced the unique Messiah. The controversy over the virgin birth stems from the attempt to understand it using common human terms and reasoning. God's ways are not reasonable because He is neither human nor finite.

Jesus participated fully in all that it means to live a human life. However, if Jesus were merely human, no matter how great, there would be no significance in drawing attention to His bodily existence. God began to live a fully human life in Jesus (2 Cor. 5:19). The Apostle Paul declared, "In Him dwells all the fullness of the Godhead bodily (Col. 2:9)." The ability of Jesus to reveal God to us and to bring salvation depends upon His being fully God and fully man at the same time. Our human minds cannot fully comprehend how Jesus can be both completely God and completely man. However the Bible shows precisely how this works out in practice.

Since no person may see God and live (Ex. 33:20), God revealed Himself to man in a tangible way through Jesus who can be seen, experienced and understood by human beings (1John 1:1-4). Jesus communicates God to man perfectly because He is the exact image of God (2 Cor. 4:4; John 1:14,18). Jesus' expression of divinity in His manhood is the key to man's discernment of God. However, Jesus' humanity was not primarily to display His divinity but to attain God's redemption of humanity. Jesus lived out His human life by experiencing all the pressures, temptations, and limitations of mankind (Heb. 2:18; 4:15; 5:2). Therefore Jesus' life is the perfect human success story. Jesus was the first born of many brethren (Rom. 8:29), showing in practice the full meaning and possibility of human life, lived in full submission and obedience to God. Jesus marked the new birth for the human race as the second Adam (Rom. 5:14-15; 1Cor. 15:45-48).

Jesus would have performed a great work if He had done no more than set a perfect example but hardly worth the miracle of incarnation. However His full humanity is also the required basis for Him to take our place and sacrificially die for us. The Bible makes this clear when it speaks of "one Mediator between God and men, the Man Christ Jesus, who gave Himself a ransom for all." Jesus' incarnation prepares Him perfectly to be the kinsman redeemer of the human race.

When He ascended to His Father after His resurrection, Jesus left behind some of the human restrictions experienced during His earthly life just as He had left behind some of His Divine attributes when He became flesh (Phil. 2:5-8). He received at that time His original divine glory (John 17:5; Phil. 2:9-11). However, the joining together of deity and humanity that marks His incarnation did not come to an end with His ascension. Jesus took His resurrected body with Him back to heaven (Lk. 24:51; Acts 1:9). In heaven now He is our divine Lord, our human leader, and the great High Priest who serves as a mediator between God and man (Heb. 3:1). Therefore, the heresies that declare Jesus to be either only human or only divine, make Jesus, God's gift for the salvation of humanity, to be common. The idea that Jesus can do nothing on the earth except through his body, the church, denies the divine attribute of Jesus' omnipresence. While Jesus works primarily through the church He is definitely not limited to only this means.

Jesus' public ministry began with His baptism at the hands of John the Baptist. John[2] preached between A.D. 27 and 28 in the lower Jordan Valley and baptized those, both Jews and Gentiles, who wished to give expression to their repentance. The descent of the Holy Spirit in bodily form like a dove (Lk. 3:22) as Jesus came up out of the water was a sign that He was the One anointed by the Spirit of God as the Servant-Messiah of His people (Is. 11:2; 42:1; 61:1). The dove that symbolizes peace, innocence, gentleness, and meekness was also a symbolic prophecy of Jesus' lifestyle. Since the dove was also used as a sacrifice of the poor, it also symbolically prophesied that Jesus would be a sacrifice for those who were "too poor to pay." The voice from heaven that declared, "You are My beloved Son; in You I am well pleased (Lk. 3:22)" indicated that He was Israel's anointed King. He was destined to fulfill His kingship as the Servant of the Lord described centuries earlier by the prophet Isaiah (Is. 42:1; 52:13).

Immediately following Jesus' baptism in the Synoptic Gospels[3] is His temptation[4] in the wilderness. This testing experience confirmed His understanding of the heavenly voice and His acceptance of the path that it marked out for Him. It also demonstrates that through use of God's Word Israel could have overcome her temptations in the wilderness and the saints today can remain victorious in all circumstances. His use of the Word of God rather than His power as God's Son is an example of both humility and the overcoming life.

Jesus' proclamation of His Kingdom of God was accompanied with works of mercy and power. These works included the healing of the sick and deliverance of those who were demon-possessed. The demons that caused such distress to men and women were signs of the kingdom of Satan. The superior strength of the kingdom of God was proved when they were cast out.

For a time, Jesus' healing aroused great popular enthusiasm throughout Galilee. Eventually the religious leaders and teachers found much of Jesus' activity disturbing. He refused to be bound by their religious ideas and traditions. He befriended social outcasts. He insisted on understanding and applying the law of God in the light of its original intention, not according to the popular interpretation of the religious leaders. He insisted on healing sick people on the Sabbath day. He believed that healing people did not profane the Sabbath but honored it. God established the Sabbath for the rest and relief of human beings (Lk. 6:6-11; Mk. 2:27). He further saw healing as the fulfillment of Messianic prophecy (Matt. 8:16-17; Isa. 53:4-5). Peter also proclaimed this view in his epistles (1 Pet. 2:24) indicating its appropriateness for the church age. Physical healing is important because it visually demonstrates the spiritual healing of redemption.

Jesus' attitude brought Him into conflict with the scribes, the official teachers of the law. Hence, they soon barred Him from preaching in the synagogues. This proved to be an example of God working to change setbacks into giant steps forward (Rom. 8:28). His move from the synagogue to the hillside and lake shore only resulted in larger crowds to listen to Him. His simple stories from daily life experiences drove home special points and made them stick in the hearer's understanding. These simple stories are parables and continue to be effective tools of preaching today.

The enthusiasm of the people when Jesus entered Jerusalem on a donkey alarmed the religious leaders. So did his show of authority when he cleared the Temple of traders and moneychangers. This was a "prophetic action" in the tradition of the great prophets of Israel. Its message to the priestly establishment came through loud and clear. The prophets' vision of the Temple as a house of prayer for all nations was a fine ideal (Isa. 56:7). However, any attempt to make it a reality would be a threat to the commonly accepted priestly privileges. Jesus' action was as disturbing as Jeremiah's speech foretelling the destruction of Solomon's Temple had been to the religious leaders six centuries earlier (Jer. 26:1-6).

The Jewish leaders attempted first to convict Him of being a threat to the Temple. Protection of the sanctity of the Temple was the one area in which the Romans still allowed the Jewish authorities to exercise authority. Nevertheless this attempt failed. When Jesus accepted their charge that He claimed to be the Messiah, the religious leaders had an occasion to hand Him over to Pilate on a charge of treason and sedition. While "Messiah" was primarily a religious title, its political meaning would be "king of the Jews." Anyone who claimed to be king of the Jews, as Jesus admitted He did, presented a challenge to the

Roman emperor's rule in Judea. On this charge Pilate, the Roman governor, finally convicted Jesus. This was the charge explained in the inscription fixed above His head on the cross. Death by crucifixion was the penalty for sedition by one who was not a Roman citizen.

With the death and burial of Jesus, the narrative of His earthly career came to an end. However, with His resurrection on the third day, He lives and works forever as the exalted Lord. His appearances to His disciples after His resurrection assured them He was "alive after His suffering (Acts 1:3)." These appearances also enabled them to make the transition in their experience from the form in which they had known Him earlier to the new way in which the Holy Spirit would relate them to Him.

CHAPTER 4

WORD OF GOD

The Word of God is holy or uncommon because it is simply the Word of the God who is righteous all together. Since it is His word, it must be holy as He is holy. Because it is His Word it must be all that He is. Jesus is also known as the Word[1] of God. John presents Him this way and points to the fact that He has always been (John 1:1-18). The expression "Word (*logos*) of God" is also used of the Bible. It is the written record of the Word (*rhema*)[2] of God that came to prophets, apostles, and other spokesmen, and which "became flesh" in Jesus Christ. Christians believe Jesus Christ was the Word of God in a unique sense. Through Jesus, God communicated the perfect revelation of Himself to mankind in fleshly form. Therefore the authority of the Bible is related to the authority of Christ and the God who is behind it.

The Bible contains two major divisions known as the Old Testament and the New Testament. The books of the Old Testament were written over a period of more than ten centuries in the Hebrew language, except for a few selected Aramaic passages. The Old Testament tells of the preparation that was made for Messiah's coming and God's self disclosure to His people. The Old Testament was the authority to which Jesus made constant appeal and whose teachings He accepted and followed. When Jesus was arrested in the Garden of Gethsemane and led away to His mock trial and crucifixion, He submitted with the words, "The Scriptures must be fulfilled (Mk. 14:49)." He saw His mission in the world as a fulfillment of the prophecies of the Old Testament which were the expressed will of the Father.

The New Testament presents the record of Jesus' life, teachings, death, and resurrection; a history of the infant church with the coming of the promised Holy Spirit; and the story of the extension of the gospel and the planting of churches during the following generation throughout the Gentile world. It also contains the written teachings of Jesus' apostles and other early Christians who applied the principles of His teaching and redemptive work to their lives. The New Testament was originally written in the Greek language over a period of about 100 years.

None of the books written after the death of the apostles are included in the New Testament, although early church officials recognized they did have some value as inspirational documents. The fact that they were written later ruled them out for consideration among the church's foundation documents. These other writings might be suitable for reading aloud in church because of their edifying character, but only the apostolic writings carried the authority of being Scripture. Only the Bible should be used as the basis of the church's belief and practice. To add other writings or consider them as equal to the Bible is to profane it. The Bible is not just another book written by men. It is the Word of God. The English word testament normally refers to a person's will, the document that bequeaths property to those who will inherit it after the owner's death. However the meaning of testament from both the Hebrew and the Greek languages is "settlement," "treaty," or "covenant." Of these three English words, "covenant" is the best meaning of the word testament. Thus, the Bible is a record of God's covenant with his people.

The old covenant is the covenant sealed at Mount Sinai in the days of Moses. By this covenant, the living and true God, who had delivered the Israelites from slavery in Egypt, promised to bless them as His special people. They were also to worship Him alone as their God and to accept His law as their rule for life (Ex. 19:3-6; 24:3-8). This event was so important to God that He established a feast day, Pentecost, as a memorial. Later He poured out on the church the Spirit of Truth on the day of this feast.

The new covenant was announced by Jesus as he spoke to His disciples in the upper room in Jerusalem the night before His death. As He gave them a cup of wine to drink, Jesus declared that this "is the new covenant in My blood (Luke 22:20; 1 Cor. 11:25)." Between the times of Moses and Jesus, the prophet Jeremiah foresaw a day when God would make a new covenant with His people. Under this new covenant, God would inscribe His laws on the hearts of people rather than on tablets of stone as at Sinai (Jer. 31:31-34). The New Testament is the written record of this new covenant of which Jeremiah spoke and was inaugurated by Jesus (Heb. 8:6-13).

Both covenants launched great spiritual movements that are actually two phases of one great Redemptive act through which God has revealed His will to His people and called for their positive response. The second covenant is the fulfillment of what was promised in the first. The first is a shadow of the second.

Behind the Bible is a thrilling story of how God revealed Himself and His will to human spokesmen and then acted throughout history to preserve His Word and pass it along to future generations. The uncommon value of the Bible and its continual authority is recorded in the words of the prophet Isaiah, "The grass withers, the flower fades, but the word of our God stands forever (Is. 40:8)."

Through study of Scripture one learns who Jesus is and is shown how to become like Him. How can he become like Him, if he does not know what He is like? Devotional studies are important, but they must result from a serious study of Scripture. The apostle Paul prayed that the Colossian saints might be "filled with the knowledge of His will in all wisdom and spiritual understanding (Col. 1:9)."

Knowing Scripture as well as obeying it are the twofold foundations of the spiritual life. James declares that believers must be "doers of the word (*logos*) and not hears only (James 1:22-25)." A godlike life produces the desire to study God's Word. Satan's attempt to take away one's desire to study Scripture is nothing less than an attempt to remove the basis of our spiritual growth and stability. It is his feeble attempt to make common the bread for one's soul.

The first significant translation of the Bible is the pre-Christian Greek translation of the Old Testament called the Septuagint. A later Latin Bible known as the Vulgate was greatly dependent on the Septuagint. The modern arrangement of the Bible with four major Old Testament divisions is due to the influence of these translations.

According to the Bible, God has made Himself known in a variety of ways. The Psalmist declares, "The heavens declare the glory of God (Ps. 19:1)." Paul writes, "For since the creation of the world His invisible attributes are clearly seen, being understood by the things that are made, even His eternal power and Godhead (Rom. 1:20)." Although God is revealed in His creation and through the inner voice of man's spirit, the primary means by which He has made Himself known is through the Bible. God has revealed Himself through His mighty acts and in the words of His messengers, or spokesmen. Either of these ways is incomplete without the other. In the Old Testament record, none of the mighty acts of God is emphasized more than the Exodus, God's deliverance of the Israelites from Egyptian bondage. As He delivered His people, God repeatedly identified Himself as their redeemer God: "I am the Lord your God, who brought you out of the land of Egypt, out of the house of bondage. You shall have no other gods before Me (Ex. 20:2-3)." The Passover feast was inaugurated to celebrate this event and to remind Israel that God had redeemed them. If they had been delivered with no explanation, the nation of Israel would have learned little about the God who redeemed His people. The Israelites might have guessed that in such events as the plagues of Egypt and the parting of the waters of the Red Sea, some supernatural power was at work on their behalf. However they would not have known the nature of this power or God's purpose for them as a people.

God also spoke to Israel, through Moses, to whom He had already made Himself known in the burning bush. God instructed Moses to tell his fellow Israelites what had been revealed to him. The God of their ancestors, Abraham, Isaac, and Jacob, was at work not some impersonal deity. God was acting on behalf of their descendants to fulfill His covenants with them. God was revealing to His people both His identity and His purpose. His purpose was to make the Israelites a nation dedicated to His service alone. This message was conveyed to the Israelites through Moses and would have been ineffective if God had not delivered them personally. In the same way, His deliverance would have been meaningless without the message. Together they constituted the Word of God to the Israelites, the saving message of the God who both speaks and acts.

This pattern of God's mighty acts and the prophetic word interacting with each other continues throughout the course of biblical history. The Babylonian captivity is a good example of this process. The prophets warned the people that if they did not change their ways, captivity would come on them as judgment. Even during the years of the captivities the prophets continued to speak, encouraging the captives and promising that God would deliver them from their plight. These prophets, including the judges, delivered God's message to Israel in Old Testament times. They were not His only messengers, however. Priests and sages, or wise men, were other agents through whom God's will was made known. The teachings of many of these messengers are preserved in the Bible.

In addition to God's revelation of Himself, God's Word also records the response of those to whom the revelation was given. Too often the response was unbelief and disobedience thus making His Word common. At other times, people responded in faith and obedience thus expressing the holiness of His Word. The Psalms, especially, proclaim the grateful response of men and women who experienced the grace and righteousness of God. These faithful people sometimes voiced their appreciation in words addressed directly to God. At other times they reported to others what God had come to mean to them. In both cases they were and are able to cause faith to come to those who believed their report (Rom. 10:17).

In the New Testament writings, revelation and response came together in the person of Jesus Christ. On the one hand, Jesus was God's perfect revelation of Himself (Heb. 1:2). He was the divine Word in human form (John 1:14). His works of mercy and power portrayed God in action, especially His supreme act of sacrifice to bring about "the redemption that is in Christ Jesus." His teaching expressed the mind of God. The words and acts of Jesus also proclaimed the meaning and purpose of His works. For example, His act of casting out demons "with the finger of God (Lk. 11:20)" was a sign that the kingdom of God had come among them. He also declared that His death, which he interpreted as the fulfillment of prophecy, was "a ransom for many (Mk. 10:45)." Through His life and ministry, Jesus illustrated the perfect human response of faith and obedience to God and His Word. Jesus performed the mighty acts of God and He spoke authoritatively as God's messenger, prophet. In fact He was the message.

The Bible is a written, authoritative record by which any teaching or theory may be judged. However, these messages were circulated in oral form for long periods of time before the writing. The stories of the patriarchs were passed from generation to generation by word of mouth before they were written. The messages of the prophets were delivered orally before they were fixed in writing. Narratives of the life and ministry of Christ were repeated orally for two or three decades before they were given literary form. The Bible owes its preservation to the fact that all these oral narratives were eventually reduced to writing. Just as God originally inspired the Bible, He has used this means to preserve His Word for future generations.

The first person in the Bible to write anything down was Moses. God instructed Moses to write as a permanent memorial His vow that the name of Amalek would be blotted out of remembrance (Ex. 17:14). From that time until the end of the New Testament age, the writing of the many books and parts of the Bible continued. Forty different writers over a total of about sixteen centuries wrote sixty-six books. The harmony of these writings demonstrates one divine source behind them. Yet each writer reflects his own style and vocabulary. The Holy Spirit so moved on these writers to inspire their words so that they are individually meaningful and infallible. It is therefore profitable for doctrine, reproof, correction and instruction (2 Tim. 2:16). The fact that cults often quote the Bible to give authenticity to their false doctrine shows the universal recognition of its uncommonness. It is necessary, however, to state that while the original text is holy and without error the editorial helps and translations are not. The original scriptures were written without punctuation or even word separation. There were no chapter divisions or verse numbers. These were added later for reference convenience and should not be considered holy.

God's provision for the preservation of the Bible is also evidence of its unique quality to man. None of the original biblical documents, referred to by scholars as the "original autographs," has survived. No scrap of parchment or papyrus bearing the handwriting of any of the biblical authors has been discovered. Before the original documents disappeared, however, they were copied. These copies of the original writings or fragments of them make up the texts on which current translations of the Bible are based. The process of copying and recopying the Bible has continued to the present. Until the middle of the 15th century A. D., all the copying was done by hand. Then, with the invention of printing in Europe, copies could be made in greater quantities by using this new process. Each copy of the Bible had to be produced slowly by hand with the old system, but now the printing press could produce thousands of copies in a short time. This made the Scriptures available to many people, rather than just the few who could afford handmade copies. Gutenburg invented the movable type printing press in 1456 A.D. so that the Bible could be more readily available to all people. Today the Bible is printed in over 286 languages. Scripture portions can be read in more than 2000 languages and dialects. It has been on the "best seller" list for decades. It is printed on special paper with special ink and leather bond so that it is durable and readable for a lifetime.

Numerous stories exist concerning the power of this written word to change men's lives. The distribution of scripture parts has become a valid means of sharing the gospel with success. During World War II, Nazi prison camps forbid the reading of the Bible and singing of hymns. Bibles and Hymnals were burned and otherwise destroyed. Prisoners risked their lives to keep the scripture by dissecting Bibles and circulating pages. Some memorized whole books of the Bible so that its words would be available to the prisoners. These words strengthened the captives enabling them to bear the hardships.

The Bible declares its holiness in many places and ways. Proverbs 30:5,6 declares that the Word of God is pure and is not to be added to. It is pure because it has been tested and refined by the Holy Spirit as fine gold. Time has proven its value. Jesus and his disciples relied on the Scriptures. Peter got out of a floating boat to walk on water because he heard the word of Jesus, "Come (Matt. 14:9)!" Paul turned from Asia to Macedonia because he received a vision from God (Acts 16:6-10). Peter associated himself with those that his fellow Israelites considered unclean because God had declared them clean in a vision (Acts 11:9-14). Jesus submitted to the cruelty of the cross because He knew the prophecies concerning the suffering servant (Isa. 53:1-12). Joshua declares that every promise God gave to Israel had been fulfilled. Not one word failed (Josh 21:43-45). Isaiah declares that God's words are always true they always preform what they have been sent to do (Isa. 55:11). Jeremiah explains why this is true when he quotes God as declaring that He is "always ready to perform My word (Jer. 1:12)."

Proverbs also warns against the adding to these sacred words. No other book or writing is to be accepted as equally authoritative. Some hold the Apocrypha[3] as sacred writings but Jesus knew of these writings and may have read them but never quoted from them. Jesus' words include more than 60 quotations from the Old Testament but not one word from these. He thus made a distinction between the two. To place them along side of the Bible or include them under the same binding is to desecrate the holy thing. Does this exclude prophecy for today? The answer is an emphatic, NO! Those who reduce this gift to preaching or exclude it all together are profaning the words of God. Prophecy today will always come under the authority of the written Word. It must not be gullibly received without testing by the Spirit who lives within the believer. To think that God has nothing more to say reduces God to something less than common for common man always has something to say even when he has nothing to say. Those who want the New Testament prophet to stand equal with the Old Testament prophet need to submit to the Old Testament judgment of death to those who are not 100% accurate. Those who would speak for God should apply Paul's words to Timothy to themselves (2 Tim. 2:15) and thus reject handling as common the words delivered to them by the Holy Spirit. The modern "prophets" who accept being only 30-40% accurate when they prophesy are walking on thin ice with God. It would be better to keep silent rather than to profane God's message or attribute a message to God that is not from Him at all.

Jesus declares that God's word is eternal (Matt. 5:18; 24:35). He asserts that all of it will endure time. Even when the earth is no more His word will remain intact and in effect. Two thousand years will soon pass since the last book of the Bible was written. It has been nearly 3500 years since the first book was written. It is still as accurate today as when first completed. The prophet Isaiah declares as quoted by Peter that "the Word (*Rhema*) of the Lord endures (stands) forever (1 Pet. 1:22-25; Isa. 40:6-8)." Jeremiah explains why the Word endures as he declares that God is always in a state of readiness to perform His Word (Jer. 1:12). God who neither sleeps nor snoozes is alertly watching over His Words to make them work for those who believe them. God also declares that His Word is always fruitful and never barren (Isa. 55:11). Not only does the Word endure but it also is continually productive and it will cause faith to come whenever it is heard. Jesus refers to this quality as He calls the Word of God, seed (Lk. 8:11). As the wheat seeds that were found in the pyramids remained viable after centuries so the Word of God is always productive for eternity for whoever finds it. Jesus says that His words are life (*zoe)* producing words (Jn. 6:63). This means that God's Word is able to bring God's quality of life into one's life. It will produce God's nature within those who believe it. God declares through the Proverbs writer that His words are life and health to those who find them (4:20-27). Finding them implies a search and a discovery. This means that the Words of God must be treated more preciously than a diamond mine for the gems found here are uncommonly valuable. Once discovered these words must be kept not on a shelf or computer disk but in your heart. As they are mixed with faith they produce. Israel heard the promise of God to give them Canaan but the sight of the giants and walled cities so over shadowed the words of their god that the words could not produce their intended result (Heb. 3:12-4:3). God's Word is not to be examined and tested but believed. There are too many Gideons who hear the Word but want a second opinion and a third before they decide to do it. God's Word is fail proof. When God delivers it, He sets the necessary power in reserve to accomplish what He says. Therefore, one must only believe it and see it produce its fruit. Zechariah was struck dumb because he dared to ask "how" with a doubtful attitude (Lk 1:11-20). Mary however asked "how" with an attitude of full dependency on God to perform His Word (Lk. 1:26-38). Zechariah prayed but did not believe that God could answer so when the angel came with the promise, he received it as though it were merely common.

When one approaches God's Word, he must never forget whose words they are. They have come from the mouth of God Himself, and they demand respect. They demand to speak for themselves. They demand that one be honest and have integrity. One must not put guesswork on the same level as the words of God because that makes them common words.

Integrity is a necessary element in interpreting God's Word. When telling someone about what a friend said, one should try to be as accurate as possible. If he is not sure about a certain point, he should say, "I think this is what he said." When one interprets God's Words, should he lose that integrity? Why do some not read the Word carefully? Why do they read between the lines, make fanciful interpretations that are more a product of his imagination than reverent study, and then insist that this is what the Word actually says? One must diligently seek to rightly divide the word of truth (2 Tim. 2:15). To treat God's Word with any less respect is to profane it.

CHAPTER 5

TITHE

'Thus all the tithe of the land, of the seed of the land or of the fruit of the tree, is the LORD'S; it is holy to the LORD. (NASU, Lev. 27:30) A tithe is ten percent or one tenth. As with the tree of the knowledge of good and evil which stood in the midst of the Garden of Eden and the City of Jericho when Israel began her entry into the Promised Land, the tithe is set apart for God. It is solely the Lord's. The act of tithing is the free will worship of God our provider by presenting to Him the tithe.

The first mention of tithing in the Bible is in Genesis fourteen when Abram gave Melchizedek, king of Salem (ancient name of Jerusalem) and priest of God Most High, a tenth (tithe) of the spoils gathered in the recent war. Jacob after his encounter with God at Luz, renamed Bethel, pledged to give a tenth (tithe) of all that God gave to him back to God (Gen. 28:18-22). The New Testament writer of Hebrews explains that Melchizedek was a type of Christ whose priestly role was outside the family of Levi and Aaron and outside the Mosaic Law. He further states that all Levi's descendants contributed tithes to Melchizedek through Abraham (Heb. 7). Jacob's commitment was also pre-Moses. Moses's Law gave details about the obligation of Israel to bring the tithe of all their increase to the storehouse of God. The tithe was to be brought with the votive gifts of their sacrifices and feast day sacrifices and offerings. Because Israel was a Theocracy the normal governmental needs were also connected to their required giving. They were required to bring additional tithes at various times to cover these governmental needs. Today, we in America call these additional requirements, taxes. They were not applied to the work of the temple but the governmental needs. The rabbis expanded the teachings on tithing to include things beyond the normal agricultural increases of the people. By Jesus' day the devout religious people tithed seeds and spices in addition to the tithe of the increase (Matt. 23:23 and Luke 11:42).

From the time of creation God has made some things Holy and off limits to humans. Adam and Eve were given full management of the garden. They were supplied with food from all the trees with one exception; the tree of the knowledge of good and evil. To violate this exclusion was to bring immediate death (Gen. 2:15-17). This tree represented man's right to choose to rule over his own destiny or to remain under the authority of God. Paul in Romans five explains that Adam's choice infected the whole human race with sin and through the sin they received spiritual and physical death. As a result of their choice to be self-ruled, Adam and Eve were driven from the garden and required to till the earth and hoe the weeds and thistles that now grew in the soil.

After the flood and God's call to Abram of Ur of the Chaldeans to go to the land of Canaan, God chose the tithe as the forbidden thing. Abram and Jacob were not cognizant of the significance of their actions but it is clear from the biblical accounts that they were recognizing that their success was by God's hand and not their own. Moses was called upon to introduce the people of God to the tithe and give them detailed instruction. When the first born of the Egyptians were killed during the tenth plague, the first born of the Israelites were protected by the blood of the lamb on the door post. God later claimed the first born of the Israelites. When God claimed the Levites as His portion of Israel, they redeemed the first born children. When God selected the tribe of Levi to be priests for the nation of Israel, He provided for their well fare by allocating His tithe to be their provision. They were promised the best of the flocks and harvest. They did not inherit a portion of the land like the other tribes. They had the cities of refuge and garden plots within these cities. In the time of the Kings, Israel and Judah became lax in their observance of the law. After the division of the kingdom, Israel, the northern kingdom, pretty much abandoned worship of the Most High God and followed after the gods of the Canaanites. Judah, the southern kingdom, continued her worship at Jerusalem. She too became lax but under Hezekiah, the reform king, worship and feast day celebrations were restored along with the tithe (2 Chr. 31:5). After the Babylonian captivity and the return to the Promised Land, Nehemiah restored the tithe (Neh. 13:12). God uses Amos to rebuke Israel for her meticulous tithing while oppressing the poor and crushing the needy (Amos 4:1-5). By the time of Malachi, the last of the Old Testament Prophets, Israel's worship of God had depreciated to the point that God was magnified more outside the borders of Israel than within it. Israel had failed to see and recognize God's great love toward her and His continual blessings because of His covenant with Abraham, Isaac, and Jacob. They had lost their honor and respect for their covenant God (Jehovah, YHWH, LORD). The priests were condemned for despising His Name through the offering of blind, lame, and sick sacrifices on the alter. God sarcastically asks, "If that isn't evil, try offering them to the governor and see if you find favor" (Mal. 1:6-8)? He called upon them to repent and serve Him with respect as priests of the LORD of Host. Failure to repent would bring a curse upon them and upon the blessings they spoke over the people. They were also cited for departing from the way (NKJV, Mal. 2:8) causing many to stumble at the law and corrupting their part of the covenant of Levi. The priest's failure caused the people to profane the covenant of their fathers. They were divorcing their Israelite wives and marrying women who worshipped pagan gods. This produced children with mixed religious beliefs and thus gradually turning away from the covenant of their fathers. As you may remember, this began during the Babylonian captivity and was first addressed through Ezra (Ezra 9 & 10). Within the nation there arose sorcerers, adulterers, perjurers, those who exploited the wage earners, widows and orphans, and those who turned away a stranger. God sends a call for repentance for their abandoning His ordinances. His instructions as to how to return to Him was to stop robbing Him of tithes and offerings. His exhortation is to "Bring all the tithes into the storehouse so that the covenant with Levi could be fulfilled. This then was a call for the people of God to honor and respect Him by respecting the forbidden thing, the tithe. God then makes an offer not found with any other of His commands or statements. Israel's failure to bring the whole tithe has brought a curse (God's judgment). God's covenant promises to a faithful Israel was His blessing. Her lack of faithfulness had brought the withdrawal of her blessing. During her faithful years the nations had viewed her prosperity and honored God. He now promises to bless Israel again for putting Him first by bringing the whole tithe. He promises to send the needed rains and destroy the pests that devour the fruit and the diseases that destroy the plants and vines. This blessing is to be great enough to exceed their need and expectation even to be considered to be immeasurable (see also Jn. 10:10 and Eph. 3:20). The Law was given to teach the people of God about the gift being brought by Messiah. Every feast was a picture of a facet of this gift and illustrated each element of the gift being purchased. The laws and regulations were meant to be a tutor of the faith relationship God desired from His creation (NASU, Gal. 3:23-26). Each sacrifice was a visual illustration of Messiah's sacrifice. Many of the regulations had to do with maintaining a good relationship with one's brothers and neighbors. The tithe, however, was meant to teach the worshipper how to fulfill the first commandment ("I am the LORD your God, who brought you out of the land of Egypt, out of the house of slavery. You shall have no other gods before Me[1].")

The contemporary church does not fully agree that the New Testament endorsees the principle of tithing and financially testing God. Nelson Bible Dictionary states within the "tithe" article: "Nowhere does the New Testament expressly command Christians to tithe. However, as believers we are to be generous in sharing our material possessions with the poor and for the support of Christian ministry. Christ Himself is our model in giving. Giving is to be voluntary, willing, cheerful, and given in the light of our accountability to God. Giving should be systematic and by no means limited to a tithe of our incomes. We recognize that all we have is from God. We are called to be faithful stewards of all our possessions[2]." While New Testament believers may not be expressly commanded to tithe, they are expressly told to seek first the kingdom of God (Matt. 6:33) and provision would follow. The author, personally, sees the tithe to be like the forbidden tree in the garden and is an indicator of ones honor and respect for his God, Jehovah-Jireh. The tithe represents one's rejection of self-rule and acceptance of the authority and majesty of his God and gives glory and honor to Him. Tithing is not an issue of the purse but an issue of the heart. Proverbs chapter three challenges: "In all your ways acknowledge Him, and He will make your paths straight. Do not be wise in your own eyes; Fear the LORD and turn away from evil. It will be healing to your body and refreshment to your bones. Honor the LORD from your wealth and from the first of all your produce; so your barns will be filled with plenty and your vats will overflow with new wine."[3] Tithing is not really about money but about who's first in one's life. Since tithing was initiated before the Mosaic Law and the New Testament does not offer any alternative, it only seems logical that this practice continued. The only instructions about giving recorded in the New Testament concerns a special offering Paul was receiving for the poor saints in Jerusalem (Acts 19-21; 1 Cor. 8:1-4; 2 Cor. 8 & 9). The tithe was always a volunteer expression of worship. Since Hebrews 7 links Melchizedek with the priesthood of Jesus and being superior to the Mosaic priesthood, the New Testament tithe would be an act of worship and without compulsion through our covenant in Jesus Christ. If tithing opened the windows of blessing for the Old Testament saints how much more should it be a window opener for the New Testament Saint. Jesus in the "Sermon On The Mount" (Mt. 5-7) taught that believers who hallow the name of their Father in heaven could expectantly ask for their daily bread (provision). He further taught His disciples to put their treasurer where they desire for their heart to be and not to be caught up in the world's system of seeking after things rather than, or in preference to God. His whole teaching on "worry" pointed to one making God subordinate to the things about which one was worrying. While Jesus never mentioned tithing, yet His purpose, in the author's opinion, reflects the purpose of tithing from Abraham to Malachi.

Moses states in Deuteronomy fourteen that the purpose of the tithe is to learn to reverence the LORD your God always (v. 23). It is an act of worship to honor Jehovah-Jireh (our provider). The giving of the tithe on a regular basis teaches one to acknowledge that our prosperity is not of our doing. When Abram recognized that his success in the battle was by God's hand not his, he was not only moved to give Melchizedek the tithe of the spoils but also to give the king of Sodom, who asked for the people taken captive, all the remaining ninety per cent. He refused to give the king the ability to claim responsibility for Abraham's wealth. Abram was only willing for God to receive that honor. The next event recorded about Abram's walk with God is God's covenant with Abram. God declared to him that He was his shield, his "exceedingly great reward" (Gen. 15:1 (NKJ)). The great reward was the promise of a son (heir) and descendants as numerous as the stars. Abram's tithing to Melchizedek opened the windows of heaven to Abram's greatest need. God also entered into a covenant with Abram which became the basis of the New Testament covenant through Jesus Christ.

CHAPTER 6

SAINTS[1]

Saints are the people who have been separated from the world and consecrated to the worship and service of God. Followers of the Lord are referred to by this term throughout the Bible, although its meaning is developed more fully in the New Testament. Consecration, setting apart, and purity are the basic meanings of the Greek word. Believers are called "saints" in Rom. 1:7 and "saints in Christ Jesus" in Phil. 1:1 because they belong to the One who provided their sanctification. Saints are also those to whom the privilege of revelation (Col. 1:24-29) and the task of ministry (Eph. 4:12) are committed.

Another term used to designate those whom God has sanctified is "People of God". All people who are part of the Covenant relationship which God has established with His chosen ones are called the People of God, laity. The idea of a separated clergy is contrary to the New Testament concept of the People of God. Those who are called to ministry gifts within the church are still sheep or People of God. The only clear difference can be seen in function not rank or superiority of quality. All the People of God are called to ministry and the leadership is required to equip them for this ministry (Eph. 4:11-16).

In the Old Testament, the nation of Israel is referred to as the people of God. The Hebrew people are the Lord's "special treasure (Ex. 19:5)," His "inheritance (Deut. 4:20)," His "servant (Is. 48:20)," His "son (Ex. 4:22-23)," His "sheep (Psa. 95:7)," and His "holy people (Deut. 14:2)". The concept of the people of God stresses the truth that Israel is God's possession because of His gracious choosing—not because of Israel's merit or worth. The phrase, the people of God, refers to the special relationship of Israel with Yahweh through His Covenant with Abraham (Gen. 12:1-3).

In the New Testament, the phrase "the people of God" is used occasionally to describe the "old Israel" (Heb. 1:25). But there is a definite transition to a new covenant and a new people of God, the church, who are now "His own special people (Titus 2:14)" and "a chosen generation, a royal priesthood, a holy nation, His own special people (1 Pet. 2:9,10)". The church is seen as the new Israel, or true Israel, of God (Rom. 9:6; Gal. 6:16), the true seed of Abraham (Gal. 3:29), and the new People of God (2 Pet. 2:9). Each person who believes in the Lord Jesus Christ is chosen of God, set apart as an object of His covenant love and faithfulness. This unusual relationship with God makes the saints uncommon. When one forgets who he is, he profanes this holy relationship. God has provided Himself with an exceptional people in whom He has invested His Word and works. Peter uses the term "chosen" to explain the process of Christ's picking the saint out of the mass of humanity (1 Pet. 2:9). This expression is used also of Messiah and angels as well as believers who receive God's favor or grace. Paul expresses a similar idea as he writes that saints are saved by grace through faith and not by works or personal merit (Eph. 2:8-9).

Saints are uniquely valuable to God. This truth first appears in the Old Testament where Moses records a conversation in heaven just prior to the creation of mankind (Gen. 1:26). The subsequent unique creation was in the image of God. They were created male and female showing that this image was not physical or biological but spiritual. Man was created with a spiritual quality not possessed by the rest of creation. When Adam and Eve sinned God promised to provide a redeemer from the seed of Eve. Humanity was cursed with sin and corruption and its lifestyle of murder and idolatry demonstrated it. The Redeemer arrived centuries later as Mary, a virgin (Luke 1:27,34,35), bore a son and named him, Jesus. He proved Himself to be the Messiah promised by God to Adam and Eve and repeated to Abraham, Isaac, and Jacob. God had to perform many miracles, supernatural wonders, to bring this to pass. He set the world in place to operate under specified laws, and then deliberately circumvented those laws to bring into being His special people.

Jesus was born without a physical father to a woman who had never had sexual intercourse with anyone. By a supernatural act of the Holy Spirit, the *Logos* was placed in the womb of Mary. The King James Version uses "conceived" but the meaning of the word is "begotten". The Holy Spirit didn't impregnate Mary with divine sperm but simply placed the Word (*logos*) into her womb similar to the implantation of a test tube embryo by modern doctors. Jesus of Nazareth proved himself to be the messiah by many signs and wonders (Acts 2:15-39). His final act of redemption took place as He lay down on a cross accepting the nails driven into His hands and feet, and suffered death on the cross. The Son of God received the sin of humanity and the resulting death sentence. Understand that Jesus was born without the knowledge of sin and death. He lived without sin. He had only zoe^2 living in Him. He did not know how to die. He was immortal. God did all this to redeem sinful man from his sin. Peter (1 Peter 1:13-23) uses the words corruptible, incorruptible and precious to identify the elements of redemption. He says saints were not redeemed with corruptible (perishable) things like money but with the precious blood of Jesus the Christ the incorruptible (imperishable) Word of God who was made flesh and dwelt among men (John 1:14). The world makes human life cheap, thirty pieces of silver to buy a slave or hire a betrayer. Assassins can be hired for mere dollars. Some drug addicts will kill for a "fix". God spent the blood of His only begotten Son for man's redemption. The Nazi Holocaust ended life because of racial prejudice. Abortionists end life for a few hundred dollars with no reason. God spent His best to purchase His people. Paul reminds the saints of Corinth and all time that they have been bought with a price (1 Cor. 6:20). The price of their redemption makes saints a rare thing and of extreme value to God. Therefore treating one's grace as ordinary is to profane the price that was paid. Paul admonishes the saint to live his life in a manner that is worthy of the gospel (Phil. 1:27-28). He further declares that this will cause him to face his adversaries without terror and so declare the eternal end of his enemies and his salvation. In Romans, Paul asks the rhetorical question: "What shall we say then? Are we to continue in sin so that grace may increase? May it never be! How shall we who died to sin still live in it (NASU, Romans 6:1-2)?

To the New Testament saints God has entrusted the revelation of the gospel (Col. 1:26). The Old Testament saints had only a clouded view of the truth and the world had and has no revelation at all. Even the angels (1 Pet. 1:12) must depend on these saints to explain to them the mystery. Peter received this mystery and Jesus declared him blessed because he received it from God and not men (Matt. 18:17). Part of the work of the Holy Spirit is to lead the saint into truth and convict the world of sin, righteousness and judgment (Jn. 16:8-13). The indwelling Holy Spirit brings a revelation of the character of God to the saint and produces that character in him as he walks in the spirit. Jesus also gives certain ones to be gifts to the Church (Eph. 4:11-16). These ministry offices are given for the nurture and equipping of the saints for the work of the ministry. The word "equipping", means to make fit, preparing, training, perfecting, making fully qualified for service. This equipping involves both repairing and conditioning. It must be remembered that these gifts are sheep like those they minister to and are not meant to control the other sheep nor enter into ecclesiastical competition. As each functions as he is gifted he will be able to properly equip the saints. This makes for a uniqueness even within each ministry gift. Notice that the gifts in 1 Corinthians 12, Romans 12, and Ephesians 4 are not the same. The gifts of Ephesians 4 are given by

Jesus to minister to His church. The gifts of 1 Corinthians 12 are given to the saints by the Holy Spirit to minister to the church as God's agents. The gifts of Romans 12 are given by the Father for the development of the saint and effectiveness of his ministry to the church. To mistreat the gift is to mistreat the Giver. To be anything other than a good gift is to profane and misrepresent the Giver. To receive the gift as ordinary or common is to profane it and the Giver. For one to treat the office as an ordinary job is to profane the call and the gift and to presume on the Giver.

Saints need to know who they are in order not to profane themselves. Israel is a perfect example of the people of God not understanding who they were and committing spiritual adultery. Under Saul the army of Israel faced the challenges of a Philistine champion named Goliath. Israel and their God were profaned by the actions of the people and the king. David, however, knew his God and who he was in Him and challenged the army to walk in a manner reflective of their covenant. In the end only David honored God and his covenant. He went against Goliath, a giant as tall as a basketball ring, with a sling and five stones and the name of his God. Goliath physically towered over David. His armor was more impressive. His coat of mail weighted about one hundred twenty-six pounds. His spear looked like a weaver's beam with a head weighing as much as a sixteen pound shot. The revelation of who he was in the covenant with Yahweh empowered David to behave uncommonly (1 Samuel 17). All saints need to receive that revelation and so act in the face of all circumstances and enemies that come against us.

Jesus prophesied that these remarkable people would do what he did and even greater things (John 14:12). The word translated "greater[3]" does not refer to works that are greater in value or consequence but greater in number and range. This was accomplished when Jesus redeemed the saints by His sacrificial death and poured out on them the Holy Spirit of promise. Paul uses the expression, ambassadors, to express this unique relationship of the saint (2 Cor. 5:20). This term expresses the fact that believers are representatives of the living God who is the ruling authority. It also implies a level of spiritual maturity not common to man since an ambassador is chosen from the ranks of the mature, experienced persons. Elsewhere in his letters to the church at Corinth, Paul speaks of the lack of spiritual insight possessed by the natural man. Their wisdom is carnal and incomplete as compared to those whom God has redeemed and therefore not sufficient for the saint's usage in facing life. As an ambassador the saint represents God and must think and act as God would. Paul instructs the saint to disregard the schemes of life as presented by the natural man and allow himself to be transformed by the renovating of his mind (Rom. 12:1). This means that the newly born saint is still thinking as the world and needs to change his way of thinking. The ambassador being mature has already begun the process of change. To act like the world and think like the world would make his new nature, common.

Jesus declared that the saint was to be light and salt in the world. Both light and salt are unaffected by their environment but rather effect their environment. Light changes the darkness to light. Salt flavors the whole of its environment. Jesus also says that the kingdom of God is comparable to yeast that changes the whole lump of dough. The saint then is a change agent in the world. Everywhere he goes or is he is to be an element of change. To be changed by his environment is to deny the power that works within him and to profane the one he represents. The saint is called to a hard task because it is not easy to be different. God however has empowered the saint with such contagion that he is capable of making others like him. The author remembers times when as a pastor he would change the whole character of a room by entering. It seemed as though each man's vocabulary was transformed as he entered the room. Jesus gave his disciples authority over all the power of the evil spirits (Lk. 10:19). That same delegated power (authority) belongs to the saint and can prohibit the evil from operating in his presence. When Jesus said that those who believe in Him would cast out demons (Mk. 16:15-18), He was not speaking figuratively nor exclusively of deliverance of individuals. He was speaking of the power that believers possess to change their world by forbidding and permitting demon activity. Believers who do not believe in demons cannot experience the fullness of this scripture neither the completeness of the saintly life. The author remembers an occasion while serving in Barbados. A demon possessed woman entered a bus and started a disruption. The author and his wife began to quietly pray and take authority over the demon refusing to allow him to disrupt. After a few moments, the demon possessed woman quieted down. Some of the passengers near the author observed the prayer and thanked the author and his wife. While Jesus indicated that many would not accept His way of life, He also declared that this world was made for those who do. He thus sent His believers out to set the world upright (Lk. 10). Paul and the early Apostles accomplished part of this and were accused of turning the world upside down (Acts 17:5-8). What had Paul done to bring this kind of statement? Paul had simply cast out a spirit of divination and loosed Philippi from the power of *Python* or *Puthon*. Thessalonica heard of it and did not want it to happen there. It happened anyway as some believed and Paul wrote two epistles to that church.

Jesus also gave the ability to change circumstances to the saints. He indicates that the problems of life can be changed if the saint will have faith in God and act with that faith by speaking to the problem (Mk. 11:22-26. He must believe that the words he speaks can and will change things and not doubt in his heart. These faith filled words are not some magical enchantment that will make the problem disappear. These are words based on one's faith in God and one's knowledge of Him and His Word. Jesus taught the saint to speak faith words to his circumstances and receive victory because God hears. He must also be free of unforgiveness for his words to be powerful. Problems can cause hurts and unforgiveness to come but the saint must remain free from harboring these resentments and unforgiveness. This is a positive lesson from the fig tree. There is also another lesson that is negative. Jesus entered Jerusalem at the shouts of the people (Mark 11:1-22). He came as a king riding on a donkey colt that had not been previously ridden. The people declared their king with shouts of Hosanna but six days later they will call for his crucifixion. When Jesus observed the erosion of temple life, He was deeply moved and cleansed the temple. The holy house of God was being treated as an annex of the common market. The religious leaders were party to the extortion of the worshippers. The temple had become so common that people used it as a shortcut between the city and the Mount of Olives. Probably the most upsetting observation was that the court of the Gentiles housed the commerce display. As a visual demonstration of God's displeasure Jesus cursed the fig tree. Israel is symbolized throughout the Bible by the fig tree. The tree Jesus chose was like Israel. There were leaves on the tree but no fruit. The fruit precedes the leaves and even though it was not the normal time for figs this tree indicated that it had fruit. Israel declared to the world that her God was the only God. She looked to the coming Messiah and proclaimed His coming but denied Him when He came. Israel was to be the source of blessing for the whole world but was sadly empty of fruit. Saints must be aware that God is never mocked or deceived. The fruit is always representative of the seed sown. No fruit indicates that no seed was sown. People who profess to be saints but do not bear fruit of change are barren fig trees. The barren church is no better than barren Israel. God has entrusted to the Church the message of reconciliation between God and man. The saint serves as a visual representation of the power of the message. He is Christ's letter to a lost and dying world (2 Cor. 3:1-3). To have crooked type or improper words or blurred letters is to profane the writer and the message.

Jesus indicated that these saints are branches of Him, the vine, and are to bear fruit accordingly (John 15:1-8). Those branches that bear sparingly will be pruned to bring out the best in them. Those, however, that do not bear fruit will be cut off and carried away. This passage helps one to see that God's grace can be resisted and the flow of life (zoe) ended. Some say that these branches represent hypocrites and professing Christians but are really not believers. Jesus's words, however, declare that His disciples were the branches (John 15:2, 5). These branches were part of the vine. They were drawing life-giving power from the vine. For some reason their ability to produce fruit was ended.

Judas was included as part of the disciples and no differentiation was made until the spirit of greed gripped him (Matt. 26:14-16). There was a definite time when Satan entered Judas (Luke 22:3) and he became the betrayer. Jesus refers to him (v12) as the son of perdition (destruction) in his prayer recorded in John 17. Jesus also says that he was the only one that God entrusted to Him while He was on earth that was lost. This clearly indicated that a saint can lose his security of Jesus' hand. Romans 10 adds to the scriptural proof of this truth. Verse 9 uses the aorist[4] Greek tense for the verbs, confess and believe. This means that there must be a clear time when one becomes a follower of Jesus. One is not physically born a Christian but must be re-born into the family of God. Verse 10 changes the verbs to present[5] tense that means that the confessing and believing must continue for the saint to receive his final salvation. The implication is that those who recant their belief in Jesus as Savior will not receive their salvation. They are apostates not backsliders who have fallen into sin. John 10 indicates that from God's point of view this salvation is a secure matter but Romans indicates that from the saints point of view he must continue to confess and believe. Jesus indicates in His discussion of the signs of the End of the Age (Matt. 24:4-14, vs13) that one must endure to the end to be saved. This is not a passive holding on but an energetic resistance while bearing up under the pressure. Therefore we see that the saint is holy and his salvation is equally uncommon. One need not continually declare his common heritage. One's salvation that is not common, however, must continually be declared and sustained by faith to be firm.

It was to His remarkable saints that Jesus gave a commission to take the gospel message to the entire world. He said in Matthew 28:18 that He has all authority on earth and in heaven now that He is resurrected. Therefore, in this authority He sent the disciples of all ages into the whole world to every race. Their task was and is to make disciples. The Greek word translated "go" is not a verb but a participle. Therefore it should be translated "as you go" or "having gone". Jesus did not tell the saints to "go"; rather He told them to "make disciples" wherever they were. This reemphasizes what Jesus taught them as He called them light and salt. To be a secret disciple then is to make common the responsibility and privilege of sainthood. Jesus said that certain signs would follow those who believe (Mark 16:15-18). Some try to disallow these verses as not present in the earliest manuscripts. However, these verses are repeated in word, form, or action throughout the New Testament. They are fully illustrated in the Church of the Book of Acts. They spoke with tongues. They cast out demons. Paul shook off a deadly asp on the isle of Malta causing the people to think he was a god. The Greek verb "take up"[6] can also be translated "remove, take away, cast away." History also records God's miraculous protection of His missionary saints in pagan lands against the ill effects of impure food and drink. Jesus did not mean for these signs to be waved as banners or used to exhibit spirituality. They are the common fruit of a saintly life in Him. God's saints are indeed marvelous creatures and very uncommon.

CHAPTER 7

SIGNS, WONDERS, AND MIRACLES

As God and His saints are uncommon so the signs and wonders that they do are equally uncommon. A sign is something that points to, or represents, something larger or more important than itself. The Bible refers to a wide variety of things as signs. By far, the most important use of the word is in reference to the acts of God. Thus, it is often linked with "wonders" or miracles. In the Old Testament most references point to the miracles produced by God to help deliver the Hebrew people from slavery in Egypt (Ex. 7:3; Is. 8:18). God gave an unusual and supernatural sign to Hezekiah to assure him that he would recover from his illness (2 Ki. 20:8-11). In the New Testament the word "sign" is linked with both wonders and miracles. Signs point primarily to the powerful, saving activity of God as experienced through the ministry of Jesus and the apostles. The word "sign" occurs frequently in the Gospel of John and points to the deeper, symbolic meaning of the miracles performed by Jesus. Throughout the Bible, one understood the true significance of a sign only through faith.

Miracles are historic events or natural phenomena that appear to violate natural laws but which reveal God to the eye of faith at the same time. A valuable way of understanding the meaning of miracles is to examine the various terms for miracles used in the Bible. In both the Old Testament and the New Testament the authors use the word "sign" to denote a miracle that points to a deeper revelation (See Is. 7:11,14; John 2:11). "Wonder" emphasizes the effect of the miracle, causing awe and even terror (See Joel 2:30; Mark 13:22). A "work" points to the presence of God in history, acting for mankind (See Matt. 11:2). The New Testament uses the word "power" to emphasize God's acting in strength (See Mark 6:7). These terms often overlap in meaning as in Acts 2:43. However they are more specific than the more general term "miracle."

The Old Testament recognized that God is the Creator and sustainer of all life. This realization permitted the Israelites the possibility of miracles. They thought of the world as God's theater for displaying His glory and love. Thus, the miracle was not so much a proof for God's existence as a revelation to the faithful of God's covenant love. When God parted the water for the Israelites, or when He saved Israel in Egypt through the Passover and other plagues, He revealed His character; and convinced the Israelites that He was working for their salvation (Exodus 12:13-14). Miracles were expressions of God's saving love as well as His holy justice.

The Old Testament authors connected miracles especially with the great events in Israel's history (i.e., the call of Abraham (Gen. 12:1-3), the birth of Moses (Ex. 1:1-2:22), the Exodus from Egypt (Ex. 12:1-14:31), the giving of the Law (Ex. 19:1-20:26), and entry into the Promised Land (Josh. 3:1-4:7)). While these miracles were for salvation, God also acted in history for judgment (Gen. 11:1-9). The plagues of the Exodus showed God's sovereign power in both judgment and salvation (Ex. 7:3-5). He was further establishing that He was God of all the earth. In parting the water, God showed His love and protection for Israel as well as His judgment on Egypt for its failure to recognize Him (Ex. 15:2, 4-10). During the wilderness journey, God demonstrated His love and protection in supplying the daily manna (Ex. 16:1-36). Another critical period in Israel's history was the time of Elijah, the champion of Israel and prophet of Almighty God. Elijah controlled the rain and successfully challenged the pagan priests of Baal (1Ki. 17 & 18). God thus revealed Himself as Lord, the Savior of Israel, and the punisher of Israel's enemies.

Miraculous wonders like these were not as frequent during the days of the writing prophets. One unusual miracle was Hezekiah's recovery (2 Ki. 20:1-21; Is. 38:1-21). Jonah and Daniel set down other miracles. Prophecy itself is a miracle. God revealed Himself during this time through the spoken and written Word of the prophets. They spoke only the truth and every word they spoke happened.

The New Testament miracles are essentially expressions of God's salvation and glory as they were in the Old Testament. Jesus explained the reason that He performed miracles when John the Baptist, who was in prison, sent some of his disciples to Jesus to see if He was the "one to come" (Matt. 11:3). Jesus told them to inform John of what He had done: "The blind receive sight, the lame walk, those who have leprosy are cured, the deaf hear, the dead are raised, and the good news is preached to the poor (Matt. 11:5)." With these words, Jesus declared that His miracles were the fulfillment of the promises of the Messiah's kingdom as foretold by Isaiah.[1] Jesus' miracles were signs of the presence of the kingdom of God (Matt. 12:28).

The Gospel of John develops and deepens the theme of the miracles pointing to the kingdom of God. John presents the miracles of Jesus as "signs" on seven occasions.[2] He thought of these miracles as pointing to deep spiritual truth, demanding obedient faith (John 2:11,23-25). Thus, Jesus' miracle feeding of the five thousand was Jesus' presentation of Himself as the true bread from heaven, Manna, the one who gives life (*zoe*) and sustenance (John 6).

Jesus's miracles were not only evidence of the nearness of the kingdom of God and God's gift of salvation but God's great love for His creation. The most unlikely people received miracles hence illustrating that the salvation of God is to those who are rejected. He healed the lame, the dumb, and the unclean, the blind, woman with the issue of blood, and lepers. Jesus brought the kingdom to all, regardless of their condition and social standing.

But Jesus' miracles were not showy exhibitions. They required faith by the recipients. An example is the hemorrhaging woman who was healed because of her faith (Matt. 9:18-26). Furthermore, Jesus expected the disciples to do miracles and rebuked them for their "little faith" and unbelief (Matt. 17:20). Their subsequent request for more faith brought rebuke and a reminder that He had given them faith to use. If they used what they had been given, they would never be in impossible situations.[3]

Jesus did not work miracles to prove His deity or His being Messiah. In fact, He clearly refused to work miracles as proofs.[4] The words of the Old Testament prophets and His death were the proof to Israel. However, Jesus' miracles do give evidence that He was divine, that He was the Son of God, the Messiah. The Acts of the Apostles is a book of miracles. Again, these miracles are a continuation of the miracles of Jesus, made possible through the Holy Spirit. The apostles worked miracles in the name of Jesus which were manifestations of God's salvation. Peter's miracles that paralleled those of Jesus contain this thread of continuity.[5] God began His church with a powerful display of miracles. At Pentecost, the Holy Spirit came on the people with great power, leading to three thousand conversions (Acts 2:1-13, 42). When Philip went to Samaria, the Spirit of God anointed him with power (Acts 8), and the same happened with Peter and Cornelius (Acts 10). God designed these powerful wonders to convince the apostles and the Palestinian church that other cultures were to be part of the church. To these were added the stunning death of Ananias and Sapphira who acted in hypocrisy before Peter (Acts 4 & 5), the church's power in prayer (Acts 4), and Paul's transforming vision (Acts 16). Miraculous powers were also present in Peter who healed a lame man, and a paralytic (Acts 3), and raised the dead (Acts 9). The apostles performed mighty miracles (Acts 5), and Peter was miraculously released from prison (Acts 12). Paul's conversion was another startling incident (Acts 9). Paul used the ability to work miracles as a sign for his apostleship (Romans 15:18-19; 2 Cor. 12:12). Thus, this ability to work miracles is not only an expression of God's salvation but also God's way of authenticating His apostles. The list of the gifts of the Spirit in 1 Corinthians 12 shows miracles were one of the means by which believers were to minister to others.

The Bible refers to God's mighty acts as "works". Creation, redemptive acts in history like the Exodus, and even wrath are referred to as God's work. Jesus Christ's work was given to Him by His Father. His task was to accomplish redemption for man on the Cross. Paul declares that believers were created for good works by God (Eph. 2:10). When the Pharisees attributed the mighty acts of Jesus to Beelzebub, they received a stern warning (Matt. 10:25; 12:24-27). Today there are some who speak against wonders and miracles and attribute them to Satan. This is to treat as common the holy acts of God. Believer's must not treat the gifts given to them as common and for show. One must always have pure motives in all their works. Some also ascribe to God, acts of sickness, calamity, and death. Since these acts are contrary to the nature of God, they not only profane Him but His holy miracles as well. Since Jesus is the personification of God's will, we can exam Jesus' lifestyle to discover the will of God. Jesus never made anyone sick but rather healed all who came to Him. He never sent a storm on people but rather stilled the storm. He refused to call fire from heaven on His opposition but told His disciples that He did not come to destroy life but to give life. Jesus' lifestyle declares these other acts to be common, common to fallen creation. To be supernatural means that it is outside the realm of the natural. Satan, an angel, is supernatural. His acts would be classified as supernatural but never as holy or uncommon. Therefore, we must be cautious in judging supernatural things.

CHAPTER 8

COVENANTS AND PROMISES

A promise is a solemn pledge to perform or grant a specified thing. God did not have to promise anything to sinful man. Because God's nature is characterized chiefly by grace and faithfulness, almost all biblical promises are those made by Him to man.

Grace prompted God to promise a new land to Abraham and through Jacob to the Israelites (Gen. 13:14-18; Ex. 12:25). His faithfulness urged Him to fulfill that promise, in spite of the nation's disobedience. Paul pointed out in Galatians chapter three, that God's faithfulness and grace are particularly evident in His promise to Abraham (verses 15-29). The work of Christ eventually fulfilled this promise. Christians should trust completely that God's promise of eternal life is secure (Heb. 9:15). However, it is not without conditions as some failed to enter the Promise Land (Heb. 3:16-4:12).

A covenant is an agreement between two people or two groups that involves promises made to each other. The idea of covenant between God and His people is one of the most important theological truths of the Bible. By making a covenant with Abraham, God promised to bless His descendants and to make them His special people. Abraham, in return, was to remain faithful to God and to serve as a channel through which God's blessings could flow to the rest of the world (Gen. 12:1-3).

Before Abraham's time, God also made a covenant with Noah (Gen. 9), assuring Noah that He would not again destroy the world by flood. Another famous covenant was between God and David, in which David and his descendants were to be the royal heirs to the throne of the nation of Israel (2 Sam. 7:12; 22:51). This covenant agreement reached its highest fulfillment when Jesus the Messiah, a descendant of the line of David, was born in Bethlehem about a thousand years after God made this promise to King David, and was proclaimed to be King of the Jews.

A Biblical covenant is much more than a contract or simple agreement. A contract always has an end date, while a covenant is a permanent agreement. Another difference is that a contract generally involves only one part of a person, such as a skill, while a covenant covers a person's total being. The word for covenant in the Old Testament also provides additional insight into the meaning of this important idea. It comes from a Hebrew root word that means "to cut". This explains the strange custom of two people passing through the cut bodies of slain animals after making an agreement with each other (Gen. 15:7-21; Jer. 34:18). A ritual or ceremony such as this always accompanied the making of a covenant in the Old Testament. Sometimes those entering into a covenant shared a holy meal (Gen. 31:54), planted a tree, or exchanged gifts. God commanded Abraham and his children to be circumcised as a sign of their covenant (Gen. 17:10-11). Moses sprinkled the blood of animals on the altar and upon the people who entered into covenant with God at Mount Sinai (Ex. 24:3-8).

The Old Testament contains many examples of covenants between people who related to each other as equals. For example, David and Jonathan entered into a covenant because of their love for each other. This agreement bound each of them to certain responsibilities (1 Sam. 18:3). The striking thing about God's covenant with His people is that God is holy, all-knowing, and all powerful; but He consents to enter into covenant with man, who is weak, sinful, and imperfect. This illustrates that covenants were often for the protection of the weaker and not for the benefit of the stronger.

The New Testament makes a clear distinction between covenants of Law and covenants of Promise. The apostle Paul spoke of these two types of covenants, one originating "from Mount Sinai," the other from "the Jerusalem above" (Gal. 4:24-26). Paul also argued that the covenant God established at Mount Sinai, the Law, is a "ministry of death" and "condemnation" (2 Cor. 3:7,9). It is a covenant that one cannot obey because of man's weakness and sin (Rom. 8:3). However, the "covenants of promise" (Eph. 2:12) are God's guarantees that He will provide salvation in spite of man's inability to keep his side of the agreement because of his sin. The provision of a Chosen People through whom the Messiah would be born is the promise of the covenants with Adam and David (Gen. 3:15; 2 Sam. 7:14-15). The covenant with Noah is God's promise to withhold judgment on nature while salvation is occurring (Gen. 8:21-22; 2Pet. 3:7,15). In the covenant with Abraham, God promised to bless Abraham's descendants because of his faith. One may consider these many covenants of promise as one covenant of grace, which the life and ministry of Jesus fulfilled. His death ushered in the new covenant under which God's grace and mercy justifies us rather than our human attempts to keep the law. Jesus Himself is the Mediator of this better covenant between God and man (Heb. 9:15).

Jesus' sacrificial death served as the oath, or pledge, which God made to us to seal this better covenant. He is determined to give us eternal life and fellowship with Him, in spite of our unworthiness. The Book of Hebrews declares, "The word of the oath, which came after the law, appoints the Son who has been perfected forever (Heb. 7:28)." This is still God's promise to any person who turns to Him in repentance and faith (Rom. 10:13). To these believers He gives the Holy Spirit as His seal or guarantee of the covenant (Eph. 1:13-14). This covenant is uncommon because it was ratified by the precious blood of Jesus. God's commitment is that for Him to break the covenant means His ceasing to exist. Therefore this covenant and all of His covenants are unbreakable by God. "For whosoever shall call upon the name of the Lord shall be saved (Rom. 10:13)." Notice the strong wording, "shall be saved." God cannot break the covenant if He is to continue to exist and since He is eternal, He cannot break the covenant. Does that mean that the person who enters into this covenant receives the blessings of the covenant regardless of what he does? An emphatic NO is the answer. The Israelite at the first Passover was required to place blood on the door posts and remain inside under the protection of the blood. The believer who has washed his sins under the blood must also remain under its protection. Romans 10:10 points out that one must continue to believe and continue to confess in order for him to receive salvation. For an individual to break this covenant means death, not physical but spiritual. The author believes that there is no longer any sacrifice for him because he now rejects it.

The Bible further declares that God's promises are always affirmative (2 Cor. 1:20). God never goes back on His word nor do His promises or covenants end. That means that the promises of God printed in the Bible are still in effect and still affirmative to those to whom He made them. Most of them are applicable to all those who believe. These promises are primarily for those who have accepted God's promise of salvation. The author lived in nations where witchcraft and idolatry are common. There were and are those who continually speak evil things and pronounce curses upon believers. The promise of Isaiah 54:17 has proven to be a protection and a hedge against these evil practices. This promise is the heritage of those who are servants of the Lord.

CHAPTER 9

REDEMPTION

Redemption is deliverance by payment of a price. In the Old Testament, it refers to redemption by a kinsman (Num. 3:49-51), rescue or deliverance,[1] and ransom.[2] In the New Testament, it refers to salvation from sin, death, and the wrath of God by Christ's sacrifice. Its root meanings refer to loosing[3] and loosing away.[4]

In the Old Testament the writers applied the word redemption to property, animals, persons, the nation of Israel as a whole, and the tithe. In nearly every instance, freedom from obligation, bondage, or danger was secured by the payment of a price, a ransom, bribe, satisfaction, or sum of money paid to obtain freedom, reconciliation, or favor. Men may redeem property, animals, and individuals (slaves, prisoners, indentured relatives) who are legally obligated to God or in bondage for other reasons. God alone, however, is able to redeem from the slavery of sin (Ps. 130:7-8), enemy oppressors (Deut. 15:15), and the power of death (Job 19:25-26; Ps. 49:8-9). The New Testament emphasizes the tremendous cost of redemption, "the precious blood of Christ" (1 Pet. 1:19; Eph. 1:7; Rom. 3:25). Paul and Peter both exhort believers to remember the "price" of their redemption as a motivation to personal holiness (1 Cor. 6:19-20; 1 Pet. 1:13-19). The Bible also stresses that the result of redemption is freedom from sin and freedom to serve God through Jesus Christ our Lord. How can one fail to rejoice, having been freed from the oppressive bondage of slavery to sin (John 8:34; Rom. 6:18), the law (Gal. 4:3-5; 5:1), and the fear of death (Heb. 2:14-15)? "Therefore if the Son makes you free, you shall be free indeed. (John 8:36)"

Blood is the red fluid circulating in the body that takes nourishment to the body parts and carries away waste. Scripture often uses the word "blood" literally referring to the blood of animals (Gen. 37:31) and of humans (1 Kin. 22:35). The Bible also uses the word figuratively meaning "blood red" (Joel 2:31) or "murder" (Matt. 27:24). The phrase "flesh and blood" refers to humanity (Heb. 2:14).

The most important biblical concept regarding blood is the spiritual significance of the blood of sacrificial animals. Although some scholars believe the blood primarily means the animal's life, most agree that blood refers to the animal's death. Most of the Old Testament passages that discuss sacrifices mention the death of the animal, not its life (Lev. 4:4-5). The Bible makes it clear that the death of a specified animal substitute was the payment or satisfaction for human sins: "For the life of the flesh is in the blood, and I have given it to you upon the altar to make atonement for your souls; for it is the blood that makes atonement for the soul (Lev. 17:11)." This sacrificial animal not only substituted for the human who brought it but it substituted for the promised Messiah who by His death on the cross would atone for the sins of humanity.

In the New Testament, this Old Testament idea of sacrifice is applied to Christ's blood. References to the "blood of Christ" always mean the sacrificial death of Jesus on the cross. Paul, Peter, John, and the author of Hebrews made references to the blood of Christ. Although all have sinned, "we have redemption through His blood, the forgiveness of sins (Eph. 1:7)."

The gospel message is the report of the redemptive work of God in Christ. Paul said that he was not ashamed of this gospel because it is the power of God for the salvation of those who will believe it (Rom. 1:16). This is a message of hope to those who are perishing. It is unlike any of the messages of manmade religions who want to make any redemption a work of man. They ignore or explain away any accountability to God for sin and eternal punishment for rejection of God's provision of salvation. This makes the sacrifice of Jesus the act of a deluded man. It renders Jesus and His work as ordinary and common. Paul exhorts the believers in Philippi to live in a manner that is in harmony with the gospel (Phil. 1:27-30). He uses a strong word "worthy" to describe the appropriate lifestyle of one who has been redeemed by the blood of Christ Jesus. He says that this lifestyle should be of such a nature that he will hear of it even though he is not in Philippi. This lifestyle is one of steadfastness. The saints were to be standing together in a spiritual unity. This is not a natural bonding of souls but a unity of kindred spirits, redeemed spirits. The Philippians needed to learn to stand together as those who were first submitted to Jesus Christ as Lord. Their unity was also to include having the same understanding of life. This is not mind control or brainwashing. Someone has said that when everyone thinks alike, no one is thinking. To be of the same mind means that one has renewed his mind to think as God thinks, to live their lives with a clear understanding of their redemption. In this particular case, the Philippians who prided themselves on being Roman citizens must be aware that they were citizens of a heavenly kingdom first. This would enable them to face persecution and be victorious. The gospel is a message of hope but it is also a message of division. Those who reject the message also reject those who accept it. Paul encourages the Philippian church to stand fast and they would be evidence of the truth of the gospel. He told them not to be terrified of their enemies. "Terrified" refers to being panic stricken. It is terror that causes a horse to run through a wire fence, being cut viciously, when he hears the rattle of a snake. It is terror in the heart of a Jack Rabbit and causes him to jump higher and higher until the coyote can run under him and catch him. It is terror that strikes the swift Impala to run scared right into the pride of lions because of an old lion's roar. Paul says that the unity of spirit and mind will enable the saints to stand fast and not panic. This would result in their enemies receiving evidence of their own final destruction. He said that it would also serve as proof of the saints' salvation. It is the gospel of the redemption of man through the shed blood of Jesus that gives such confidence and assurance in the midst of persecution. To live as though one is likely to fail or must present a ledger sheet of good works at the final judgment is to render the redemption of God of no effect and makes it common. To remain quiet about what God has done for us reflects our lack of understanding of the greatness of Jesus' death on the cross. To fail to tell others of this work is to reduce it to the level of any other story. Paul goes on to promise that there would be suffering to come as a result of one's faith in Christ. This suffering would not render the saint powerless, however, nor defeated. He would emerge victoriously because of the power of the redemption of God. The Psalmist reflects this understanding even though the work was not yet completed. He says, "The Lord is on my side; I will not fear. What can man do to me (Psa. 118:6)?" If David could write these words how much more one who has been cleansed by the precious blood of Jesus. Paul's conclusion to the eighth chapter of Romans adds his words of encouragement to the church in Rome who would suffer under Nero. God's love can never be separated from us who are in Christ Jesus. Oh what power the redemption of man holds for him. There is nothing like it of any natural means. It is truly uncommon.

CHAPTER 10

MANKIND

The Bible begins with declaration of God's creation of this world and its various elements including man (Gen.1). It further states that man was created from the dust of the earth in the image and likeness of God (Gen. 2:7). The author of Hebrews, states that God's creation started with nothing (the invisible) to bring into existence the visible (Heb. 11:3). It is this author's belief that God then took the dust He had previously created and formed the first man. He did not form him from a pre-existing animal or lower life form. Some interpret this verse symbolically saying that God modified a higher sub human life form through evolution and then gave this new life form a soul and called it man. The fact that we now exist is obvious even though there are many theories as to how we came into being and when. Biblical scholars vary in the time of origin with some placing it as late as 4004 B.C. and others anywhere from 1,000,000 to 50,000 years ago.

There are disagreements among scientists and among theologians as to whether man has a body and soul (dichotomy) or body, soul and spirit (tripartite). While there are scriptures that use "soul" to include "spirit" (Matt. 10:28; 16:26; 1 Pet. 1:22) there are also scriptures that clearly show a distinction (1 Thess. 5:23; Heb. 4:12). For the author this leaves only one real answer: man is a tripartite being. Nonetheless, man is a whole being and unable for these three parts (body, soul, and spirit) to act independently; he acts as a unit. The author who is a Trinitarian sees his tripartite being as evidence of man's creation in the image and likeness of God.

Unlike the rest of creation, man was created to have communion and fellowship with God. While in the Garden of Eden he met and walked and talked with God (Gen. 2:15-17). Man was also created to do God's will and work. He was to exercise dominion over the rest of creation (Gen. 1:26-28). Man enjoyed his work. It was pleasant and rewarding. God had forbidden man from eating of only one tree in the midst of the garden. The exercise of his freewill led to man's sinning and breaking fellowship with God. God's response was to establish covenants with men whereby He ultimately sent the Redeemer-Jesus to reconcile man to God and re-establish the fellowship and communion. The fall of man (sin) turned this task into a curse. All creation now awaits man's restoration (Rom. 8:19-23). Man was also created to worship and serve his creator. He reaches his highest potential when he fulfills his created purpose. This sets him apart from the rest of creation. He is uncommon.

This uniquely created being, man, procreated unique offspring. Eve was unique from Adam. Their children were also unique. There is no other person exactly like another. Even identical twins are not exactly alike. As was stated earlier, God gives gifts to each person. These gifts immediately become unique because they have been given to unique persons. It is unreasonable to expect people to be alike and do things exactly alike. Groups that seek to make everyone in them exactly alike just make the uncommon common. It is imperative for us to celebrate our uncommonness and applaud our differences. When we recognize our differences we acknowledge the uncommonness of mankind. This is not to minimize or ignore the need for setting rules for standardizing appropriate and inappropriate behavior. God's establishment of governments (Rom. 13:1) and requirement for mankind to be subject to this authority emphasizes the need for enforcement of these rules. The Ten Commandments not only set a standard concerning man's relationship with God but also man's relationship with one another.

CHAPTER 11

FAITH

It is obvious from Hebrews 11 that faith is an uncommon thing. "Now faith is the substance of things hoped for, the evidence of things not seen (v1)." The English language however uses the word "faith" in such a way as to make it very common. English usage brings us to the understanding that there are two kinds of faith, natural and spiritual or biblical. Natural faith is common to all mankind but is very much connected to the natural senses. This natural faith is based on empirical reason, sensual observations and human knowledge. Paul makes it clear that there are some things that the human reason considers foolish but are really beyond the carnal understanding. He says that these spiritual things are only spiritually discernible (1 Cor. 2:14) thus requiring Biblical faith. Only with spiritual faith can one believe that God created the world with words He spoke and that the visible appeared from the invisible (Heb. 11:3). Only spiritual faith can believe God's promises and receive a child from a wife who is 90 years old while he is 100 years (Heb. 11:11). Only spiritual faith can believe that a wall thick enough for houses to be incorporated in it would fall down by walking around it once each day for six days and on the seventh doing it seven times and shouting for victory (Joshua 6:1-26). To the natural mind that is pure foolishness yet history records that these things happened. This spiritual faith is uncommon to mankind because it is God's faith given to all saints (Romans 12:3). In Titus 1:4 (NKJV, "To Titus, a true son in our common faith: Grace, mercy, and peace from God the Father and the Lord Jesus Christ our Savior."), Paul refers to a common faith between he and his son, Titus. This faith is NOT natural faith but faith common to all saints of God. It is therefore not unclean but at the same time shared by (common to) all who believe in the Lord Jesus Christ. It is this kind of faith that comes by hearing the Word (*rhema*) of God (Romans 10:17) and is essential to make God's grace work in the process of one becoming a Christ follower (Ephesians 2:8,9). This chapter will address itself only to spiritual faith.

Before we can understand the uncommonness of faith we must understand what faith is. Strong's Dictionary[1] has this definition: "4102 *pistis* (piś-tis); from 3982; persuasion, i.e. credence; moral conviction (of religious truth, or the truthfulness of God or a religious teacher), especially reliance upon Christ for salvation; abstractly, constancy in such profession; by extension, the system of religious (Gospel) truth itself: KJV—assurance, belief, believe, faith, fidelity."

Nelson's Bible Dictionary[2] includes this definition of faith: "Faith is a belief in or confident attitude toward God, involving commitment to His will for one's life." Faith can be defined as a trust in or adherence to a word of God. It is a sincere conviction that God's word (*rhema* or *logos*) is ever true and fully trustworthy. It can also be defined as action based on what one believes. James says that faith that does not have corresponding action is dead (James 2: 14-18). Faith then must produce a practical application of what we have heard from God. Faith is made uncommon by its relationship to God's Word. "So then faith comes by hearing, and hearing by the Word (*rhema*) of God (Rom. 10:17)." The word "word" is not referring solely to the Bible but would include God's personal communication with an individual. Faith then is based on what God says not what anyone else thinks or says. We can have confidence in our confessions of faith when they are based on God's word. Neither does faith come from experience nor from what someone tells us of their experience. It comes from believing what God has said. Since God's Word (*logos*) says that we are "saved by grace through faith (Eph. 2:8-9)"; we are "sanctified by faith (Acts 26:18)"; we are "justified by faith (Rom. 5:1)"; we are "kept through faith (1 Pet. 1:5)"; we have "access by faith into this grace (Rom. 5:1)"; and "without faith it is impossible to please God (Heb. 11:6), it would be foolish to treat it commonly. The author is saddened when he hears a Christ follower confess his faith for something to occur but has no word from God to support his "faith". Even more saddening is when the faith confession is obviously contrary to what the Bible declares.

From where then does faith come?

"So then faith comes by hearing, and hearing by the word (*rhema*) of God (Rom. 10:17)." As previously explained faith requires a word from God. Faith does not exist without this word. "For I say, through the grace given to me, to everyone who is among you, not to think of himself more highly than he ought to think, but to think soberly, as God has dealt to each one a measure of faith (NKJV, Rom. 12:3)." This Scripture makes it clear that spiritual faith is a gift from God and the context clarifies that "each one" refers to those who are believers. Jesus told Peter and the other disciples that they should have God's faith: "So Jesus answered and said to them, 'Have faith in God (Mark 11:22).'" In the *Textus Receptus* and *Nestle Greek* texts "in" is not present and "God" is in the genetive case (possessive case in English). That indicates that Jesus said that His disciples were to have God's faith or God's kind of faith. It appears obvious that if faith is given by God, it would of necessity have to be His kind. God does not give common things because He does not have anything common because He is uncommon. God's faith does not depend upon what it can see or measure empirically. God's faith is spiritual faith which calls things into being that do not already exist. He did this in creating the world. He said it and it appeared (Gen. 1:2-31). The writer of Hebrews says: "By faith we understand that the worlds were framed by the word of God, so that the things which are seen were not made of things which are visible (Heb. 11:3)."

Who has this faith?

Romans 12:3, referred to above, clearly indicates that God gives the measure of faith to Christ followers. Paul wrote the book of Romans "to all who are in Rome, beloved of God, called to be saints . . . (NKJV, Rom. 1:7)". Paul in Romans 12:1 further qualifies the recipients of this measure of faith as being "brethren". Further evidence that it is the believers who receive the "measure of faith" is seen in that unbelievers are referred to as *apistos*[3] (literally "no-faith"). Jesus said to Thomas, "Reach your finger here, and look at My hands; and reach your hand here, and put it into My side. Do not be unbelieving, but believing (NKJV, John 20:2)." Thomas had expressed that he would only believe when he could see, natural faith, but Jesus called upon him to exercise spiritual faith and blessed all those who would exercise spiritual faith without having to see or touch. Thomas' natural faith was called "no-faith" or "faithless" or "unbelieving" by Jesus. Thomas is being challenged by Jesus to move from the realm of unbelief (*apistos*) into the realm of faith (*pistos*). Paul writes to Titus, "To the pure all things are pure, but to those who are defiled and unbelieving nothing is pure; but even their mind and conscience are defiled (NKJV, Titus 1:15)." There are many other Scriptures that reveal that God considers those who reject Jesus as "unbelievers" (*apistos*).[4] Therefore, only Christ followers can have God's kind of faith.

How much faith does a believer receive?

Some say that there are different amounts of faith dispersed to each believer, but Rom. 12:3 reveals a different understanding. The King James Version inserts the word "the" before "measure of faith" to carry along the meaning of the word "measure"[5]. The word "measure" identified a specified amount that would not have varied. Just as God gives each human the same amount of muscles. These muscles are weak and undeveloped when one is first born. Some people do body building and develop their muscles and their muscles become powerful and big. Others do nothing special and their muscles develop but aren't as big nor as powerful. Notice, however, that they both have the same measure (number) of muscles on their skeleton. Unfortunately the English language uses the same word "muscles" to identify both the muscle itself and its development. Faith is like that. God gives to each believer the same faith but some develop it more than others. The Bible compares this development by referring to those who have "little faith" and to those who have "great faith". To have "little faith" is to have puny, undeveloped, or under developed faith. The centurion in Matthew 8 is described by Jesus as having "great faith" (v10). The greatness of his faith is seen as he pleads for his servants healing and Jesus said, "I will come and heal him (v7)." The centurion's response revealed his great faith. He said, "Lord, do not trouble Yourself further, for I am not worthy for You to come under my roof; for this reason I did not even consider myself worthy to come to You, but just say the word, and my servant will be healed. For I also am a man placed under authority, with soldiers under me; and I say to this one, 'Go!' and he goes, and to another, 'Come!' and he comes, and to my slave, 'Do this!' and he does it (NASU, Luke 7:6-8)." The centurion's faith was great because he believed that Jesus could and would do what Jesus said He would do (heal the servant). When Peter walked on the water he was exercising "great faith" (Mt. 14:28-31). He heard Jesus call him to come to Him. He got out of the boat and started toward Jesus. This is "great faith"! Then he began to see the boisterous wind and began to sink because he began to doubt he could walk on the water to Jesus. Jesus' word, "come", hadn't changed but now Peter doubted that he could do it. Peter's faith had atrophied but had not vanished or shrunk. His "great faith" had become "little faith".

The author had a dream/vision where he saw a man building a rock wall. He labored to wheelbarrow large rocks to the wall. He put mortar down and then lifted the rocks in place. Each night after he went home an impish man came along with a pick and picked at the mortar. When he came to soft mortar he would pick frantically until the rock fell out of the wall. The next day the worker would replace the rock and mortar before he continued building the wall. That night the man with the pick returned and picked away at the mortar. When he found a soft place he would pick faster until the rock fell. This repeated several times and the dream/vision ended. When the author wakened he asked God about this dream/vision. The explanation he received was: "the wall represented his life and the rocks represented the words of God that he had received and the mortar represented his faith concerning these words." Every word one receives from God will be followed by a test of one's acceptance and belief of that word. James tells us to count it all joy because this testing of our faith will produce patience which in turn brings maturity (Jas. 1:2-4).

Earlier we discussed the uncommonness of covenants with God. God's covenant with Abram (Gen. 12) included a promise of a homeland (Canaan) for his descendants. God repeated this promise and covenant with Isaac (Gen. 26) and Jacob (Gen. 28). When Moses was preparing to lead Israel out of Egypt, God reminded Moses and Israel through Moses of His covenant and promise of Canaan (Ex. 6). The exodus from Egypt was the beginning of a journey back to Israel's Promised Land. After numerous miracles, Israel arrived at Kadesh Barnea and prepared to invade Canaan (Num. 13). They sent in spies before the invasion (Their faith was high. They were acting on God's promise). They discovered that this was a marvelous land. The spies carried back a branch with one cluster of grapes that took two men to carry it on a pole stretched between them. They brought back figs and pomegranates too. They also reported walled cities with giants inhabiting them. These giants struck fear in the spies' hearts. They saw themselves as insects compared to these giants. Ten of the spies concluded that Israel could not successfully invade the land. However, two spies, Joshua and Caleb, declared that they should go up and possess the land because they were well able (NJKV, Num. 13:30). Israel voted with the ten spies and refused to enter. God judged their faith and only Joshua and Caleb were permitted to possess the Promised Land. The others died in the 40 years of dessert wanderings. The writer of Hebrews writes of this incident: "For who, having heard, rebelled? Indeed, was it not all who came out of Egypt, led by Moses? Now with whom was He angry forty years? Was it not with those who sinned, whose corpses fell in the wilderness? And to whom did He swear that they would not enter His rest, but to those who did not obey? So we see that they could not enter in because of unbelief (NJKV, Heb. 3:16-19)."

God expects us to believe His every word. Oh, how we disrespect Him when we question His word. Our faith in His word will remove the mountains of obstacles that face us and seek to distract us and discourage us. When we believe His word, we see these mountains removed from before us and a clear path provided to see the promise of His word. God is pleased with our faith in His word. Joshua and Caleb who passed the test at Kadesh Barnea continued to live by faith. Some forty years after the test they were faced with possessing the land that God promised them and all of Israel. Their first obstacle was a flooded Jordan River. God gave Joshua a plan and Joshua executed the plan as instructed. The priests stepped into the flood waters and they parted and all of Israel walked across. Then they encountered their first walled city, Jericho. God again gave Joshua a plan. They were to march around the city once each day for six days. On the seventh day they were to march around the city seven times, beat on their pots and pans, shout for joy and celebrate their victory. Then the walls of this great city would fall down. These walls were so thick that people lived in houses inside the walls. So that the people would know that God captured this great city the walls fell before them. This was Joshua's first victory. He went on to defeat thirty-one kings to possess the land. When Joshua distributed the land among the twelve tribes, they had to possess and inhabit their territory. Caleb was given Hebron and Debir as his inheritance. Hebron was possessed by the descendants of Anak. Anak was the father of the giants encountered 40 years earlier as the spies went into the land. Caleb drove the three sons of Anak out of Hebron and possessed the land (Jos. 15:13-19). Caleb was about eighty-five years at this time. He was rewarded for his faithfulness.

CONCLUSION

It has been the author's purpose to challenge the reader to examine his respect for the Holy things of God. It is easy to lapse into religion as Peter did and call the things God has cleansed common. Sometimes we are shocked into awareness when God challenges us. Peter learned his lesson with the sheet and the animals. It enabled him to invite the men sent by Cornelius into Simon's house and lodge them overnight and accompany them back to Caesarea. Upon arriving he was able to declare that God does not show partiality. He welcomed the believing gentiles into the church and declared that "in every nation whoever fears Him and works righteousness is accepted by Him (Acts 10:35)". Paul said it this way: "For there is no distinction between Jew and Greek, for the same Lord over all is rich to all who call upon Him. For "whoever calls on the name of the LORD shall be saved (NKJV, Rom 10:12-13)."

It should also be noted that one must keep alert so that he doesn't slip back into the old natural patterns. Paul reports in Galatians 2:11-13 that when Peter came to Antioch, the missionary center of the early church, he dined with the Gentile believers but when his fellow Jewish believers from Jerusalem came to Antioch, Peter withdrew and separated himself because he feared the Judaizers. Other Jewish Christians in the Antioch church including Barnabas also withdrew. Paul accused them of playing the hypocrite. Sometimes one finds himself being influenced by those with whom he is associating and their attitudes toward the uncommon things rubs off on us. We live in a fallen world and the principles of this world are many times contrary to God's attitude toward life. Paul warns that they can take us captive and cheat us out of the great things God is promising us (Col. 2:8). Sometimes it is the legalism of religion that robs us of the most. It is imperative that we continually check ourselves and keep our mind renewed to God's way of thinking. His ways are so liberating. He never asks anything of us or separates anything from us but the things that are for our good. His promise is that He will never withhold any good thing from us. Anything He forbids or declares Holy is for our good and is deserving of our gratitude and honor.

ENDNOTES

INTRODUCTION

1 Common or unclean is a translation of *koinos* (koy-nos') which means: common and is translated in the KJV as common, defiled, unclean, unholy.

2 King James Version of the Bible. Unless otherwise indicated all quotes will be from the KJV.

3 *koinos*; Strong's # **2839**; probably from 4862; common, i.e. (literally) shared by all or several, or (cer.) profane: KJV—common, defiled, unclean, unholy.

4 *akathartos*; Strong's # **169**; from 1 (as a negative particle) and a presumed derivative of 2508 (meaning cleansed); impure (ceremonially, morally [lewd] or specially, [demonic]): KJV—foul, unclean.

5 *katharizo*; Strong's # **2511**; from 2513; to cleanse (literally or figuratively): KJV—(make) clean (-se), purge, purify.

6 *koinoo*; Strong's # **2840**; from **2839**; to make (or consider) profane (ceremonially): KJV—call common, defile, pollute, unclean.

Chapter 1—YHWH

1 Strong's number—**6663**

2 Spiros Zodhiates, *The Hebrew-Greek Key Study Bible, Lexicon to the Old and New Testaments* (1st ed.; Chattanooga, TN: AMG Publishers, 1984), p 1630.

Chapter 2—HALLOWED BE THY NAME

1 Mt. 6:9

2 Strong's # 410 *'El* + # 7706 *Shadday*

3 Gen. 12:8; 13:4; 26:25; Ex. 3:15

4 Strong's #3045 *yâda*

5 Ex. 5:1; Jos. 7:13; Isa. 17:6
6 Jos. 22:22
7 Pubilius was the Roman Magistrate on Malta.

Chapter 3—JESUS CHRIST

1 Ps. 110; Is. 32:1-8; Amos 9:13
2 Matt. 3:13-17; Mark 1:9-11; Luke 3:21-22; John 1:29-34
3 Matthew, Mark, and Luke
4 Matt. 4:1-11; Mark 1:12-13; Luke 4:1-13

Chapter 4—WORD OF GOD

1 *logos*; Strong's # **3056**; from 3004; something said (including the thought); by implication a topic (subject of discourse), also reasoning (the mental faculty) or motive; by extension, a computation; specifically (with the article in John) the Divine Expression (i.e. Christ): KJV—account, cause, communication, X concerning, doctrine, fame, X have to do, intent, matter, mouth, preaching, question, reason, + reckon, remove, say (-ing), shew, X speaker, speech, talk, thing, + none of these things move me, tidings, treatise, utterance, word, work.
2 *rhema*; Strong's # **4487**; from 4483; an utterance (individually, collectively or specifically); by implication, a matter or topic (especially of narration, command or dispute); with a negative naught whatever: KJV—+ evil, + nothing, saying, word.
3 Apocrypha are writings in Greek written during the silent years between the Testaments. They are not considered inspired.

Chapter 5—TITHE

1 Exodus 20:1-3 (NASU)
2 Nelson's Illustrated Bible Dictionary, Copyright (c)1986, Thomas Nelson Publishers
3 Prov. 3:6-10 (NASU)

Chapter 6—SAINTS

1 *hagios*; Strong's # **40** ; from *hagos* (an awful thing) [compare 53, 2282]; sacred (physically, pure, morally blameless or religious, ceremonially, consecrated): KJV—(most) holy (one, thing), saint.
2 *zoe*; Strong's # 2222 from 2198; life (literally or figuratively): KJV—life (-time). Compare 5590.

3   *meizon*; Strong's # **3187**; irregular comparative of 3173; larger (literally or figuratively, specifically in age): KJV—elder, greater (-est), more.

4   aorist tense always means punctiliar action (point-action)

5   present tense always indicates linear action (durative or continuous action)

6   Greek verb *airo*—see Matt. 14:12; Luke 11:52; 1 Cor. 5:2; Eph. 4:31

Chapter 7—SIGNS, WONDERS, AND MIRACLES

1   Isa. 24:18-19; 35:5-6; 61:1

2   John 2:1-11; 4:46-54; 5:1-18; 6:1-15; 6:16-21; 9:1-41; 11:1-57

3   Matt. 17:20; Lk. 17:5-10; Mk. 11:22-24

4   Matt. 4:1-11; 12:38-42; Luke 4:1-13; 11:29-32

5   Luke 7:22; 5:18-26; 8:49-56; Acts 3:1-16; 9:32-35; 9:36-42

Chapter 9—REDEMPTION

1   *padah*; Strong's # **6299** To release, preserve, rescue, deliver, liberate, cut, loose, sever; to free; to ransom. KJV-X at all, deliver, X by any means, ransom, (that are to be, let be) redeem (-ed), rescue, X surely.

2   *peduwth*; or *peduth*; Strong's # **6304** from 6299; distinction; also deliverance: KJV—division, redeem, redemption. See Psa. 111:9; 130:7; Isa. 50:2.

3   *lutrosis*; Strong's # **3085**; from 3084; a ransoming (figuratively) or loosing. It signifies a release from slavery or captivity brought about by a paying of a price: KJV—+ redeemed, redemption.

4   *apolutrosis*; Strong's # **629**; from a compound of 575 and 3083; (the act) ransom in full, i.e. (figuratively) riddance, or (specially) Christian salvation; a release secured by the paying of a ransom, a deliverance, or a setting free: KJV—deliverance, redemption.

Chapter 11—FAITH

1   Biblesoft's New Exhaustive Strong's Numbers and Concordance with Expanded Greek-Hebrew Dictionary, Copyright © 1994 by Biblesoft and International Bible Translators, Inc.

2   Nelson's Illustrated Bible Dictionary, Copyright ©1986 by Thomas Nelson Publishers

3   Strong's definition of # **571** *apistos* (ap'-is-tos); from 1 (as a negative particle) and 4103; (actively) disbelieving, i.e. without Christian faith (specially, a heathen); (passively) untrustworthy (person), or incredible (thing): KJV—that believeth not, faithless, incredible thing, infidel, unbeliever (-ing). Thayer's definition of Strong's

 # 571 *apistos*-1) unfaithful, faithless, (not to be trusted, perfidious) 2) incredible; used of things 3) unbelieving, incredulous without trust (in God)

[4]   Matt. 17:17; Lk. 12:46; Acts 26:8: 1 Cor. 6:6; 7:12-15; 10:27; 14:22-24; 2Cor. 4:4; 6:14-15; 1 Tim. 5:8

[5]   Strong's definition of **# 3358** *metron* (met'-ron); an apparently primary word; a measure ("*metre*"), literally or figuratively; by implication a limited portion (degree): KJV—measure. Thayers' definition of **# 3358** *metron*-1) measure, an instrument for measuring a) a vessel for receiving and determining the quantity of things, whether dry or liquid b) a graduated staff for measuring, a measuring rod c) proverbially, the rule or standard of judgment 2) determined extent, portion measured off, measure or limit the required measure, the due, fit, measure

Edwards Brothers Malloy
Oxnard, CA USA
July 24, 2014